A SEA OF MOUNTAINS

A Sea of Mountains

Accounts of my Life

BERNARD ROY DESJARDINS

Sarah Russell Spray

Sea Spray Books

Contents

FOREWORDS

INTRODUCTION

1	Dry Point - Point Sec	8
2	Building Ships at Point Sec	13
3	The Desjardins of Point Sec	20
4	Grandfather's Second Family	29
5	Life at Point Sec	32
6	Going West	37
7	La Porte: The First Civilized Camp in Colorado	45
8	Then Came the Round-Ups	55
9	Marriage	63
10	Return to Point Sec	67
11	The Panic of 1893	71
12	Another Mining Excitement	76
13	The Cripple Creek Fire	80
14	The New Town	83
15	The Rocky Mountains	86

16	Life in Colorado	94
17	Vacation out East	97
18	The Deer Hunt	100
19	The State of Colorado	110
20	A Sea of Mountains	114

Acknowledgments   125

Forewords

My great-grandfather Bernard Desjardins' memoirs have always been the cornerstone of my project to publish the collected writings of my family - now the Sea Spray Books project. I could not allow his vivid "Accounts of my Life", to simply gather dust on the family bookshelf. It is my hope that with this publication, Bernard's tales of hardship, adventure, and family bonds will find a wider audience and their place in North American history. Although some of his language and opinions are dated, I have not softened them for a modern audience as I believe it is important to preserve his authentic voice and record of the era. My first cousin once removed, David Desjardins Hume, also published the memoirs privately in 2010, but a private publication can only get so far, and few copies remain. With gratitude to my Hume cousins and for the sake of completeness, I include David's foreword below.

Sarah Russell Spray, November 2023

When I was about four or five years old, I became aware that I had a grandfather and that I had inherited his family name, Desjardins, which was also my mother's maiden name. My two older brothers and I once went to visit him in Denver. It was an exciting and lengthy excursion by train from New Milford, Connecticut, through a change of trains in Chicago and on across the great North American continent to the great barrier of the Rock Mountains. Our mother and the three small boys occupied a "drawing room" which was set up for Mother's bed and fold-down Pullman bunks for the three of us. We would thread our way through a lengthy single file on our way to the diner, several railcars farther back along the train, where we would be served by a smiling black waiter, who provided us with quite wonderful meals for the several days that it then took to traverse the Great Plains.

Once, we crossed from one car to the next, and were surprised to find that the doors in the vestibule had been left open, and we were rattling along on a lengthy bridge over a swollen river. It was probably the Mississippi. We found it thrilling, but Mother, who was always terrified of heights, grasped as many small hands as she could and sent for the conductor.

Without further such adventure, we eventually got to Denver, where we were greeted by "Papa" Desjardins and settled in at #1177 York Street, a house he had designed and built himself.[1]

Papa came East to visit us several times in the 1930's. Once on Long Island, when we vacationed in Remsenburg, I became his roommate in the small house. My recollection is that he snored mightily.

On another visit, he laid out the brick piers of a 16-by-24-foot workshop for his grandsons (and his son-in-law), whom he felt should be building something useful or attractive, and not solely confined to book learning. Equipped with T.J. Hume's elaborate Hammacher Schlemmer workbench and many Hume family tools, the little "shop" did much to extend the useful education of his grandsons.

He was a generous and capable craftsman who delighted in his children and grandchildren. He spoke only French until his late teens, but these memoirs show that he had gained a wonderful mastery of English by the time he moved permanently to Colorado. His son-in-law, Nelson Hume, admired his compositional skill, as it revealed his talent as a narrator in English.

David Desjardins Hume, October 2010

---

[1] Having several times pledged much of what he had to financing other projects, he took care to keep the title to 1177 York Street in his wife's (or his children's) names, so that the family homestead could never be seized in a moment to satisfy some hungry partner in a time of depression.

Introduction

Denver, Colorado, September 22, 1931.
About two years ago I wrote the following story. Not feeling certain about it being of special interest, I laid it aside. Then, some time ago, upon looking it over, I decided to send it to my son-in-law, Dr. Nelson Hume, and a few days later I received from him the following letter:

"I cannot tell you how pleased I was to receive the copy of your story of Dry Point. Last night May and I sat down together in the living room, and I read it aloud. She had already read it once over by herself and could not wait to hear it again.

Aside from the tremendous interest the story has for us because it is a family story, I cannot help looking upon it from the literary point of view. I do not think you realize what a fine job you have done in presenting a narrative. It has everything that a good narrative ought to have. It is swift in its flow, vivid in its descriptions, and very human in the presentation of people. It arouses interest and arouses sympathy for the people. You get to like them by reading about them; you get to like the surroundings that are described; you get most interested in the fates of all these people now so long dead.

The part that I like about the whole narrative is its astonishing ease. There is another quality very difficult to get into narrative for any writer, and you have got it down well, it is intimate and personal without being self-conscious or conceited. Your command of language is excellent, not too wordy, by which I mean that you have used the right word in the right place, having made it strong. Moreover, you have a quality very hard for a writer to acquire, which is the giving of a definite picture of what you are talking about. I can see that ship going down off the shores of Saint Pierre. I can see the old man working in his shop on the pier, making those beautiful clean white tubs. I can see a pursuit of the white whale, or porpoise as you call it; the eels squirming in the small puddles, the range of hills back of the riverside farms, the stone mill with its aged water wheel, the arrival of Florien with his blue-eyed bride, the stern father deciding their fate, the loss of the yacht on the way to Murray Bay, and the strong mother, having lost her children, swimming ashore.

May and I will treasure that manuscript and will read it to our boys, and they will be proud to know that the blood of those men flows in their veins. From them they should have the inheritance of independence, enterprise, and strong character.

May and I, after we had finished reading the manuscript, spent an hour talking it all over and bringing back to our own minds our recent visit to the scene of that vivid story."

Bernard Desjardins, successful builder and architect in Denver, circa 1875.

Hume Family Archives

Chapter 1

Dry Point - Point Sec

A true story of a peaceful and once-happy village that is no more.

This village grew from one man's activities and enterprises. Not that this is different from the starting of any communities which are usually started in that manner, only they generally become a mixed population. But in this case, the growth and development became like one plant set out and cared for, that spreads, and blooms, then, loved by all, the time comes when the natural source supplying it fails, and it withers and perishes, *only to be remembered.*

* * * *

On the St. Lawrence, 100 miles east of Quebec, there is a chain of mountains and hills bordering a short distance from the sea, for the St. Lawrence at this point is really a gulf, or branch of the sea, with the ocean tides rising about twenty feet at this place. The mountains and hills here are in some parts very close to the sea, in other parts leaving a space of a mile or more of level land, now well cultivated farms. A part of this mountain chain forms a crook in the shape of a fishhook, coming very close to the sea. This was called Point Sec or Dry Point, presumably from forest fires on that point which had left it with dry timber.

Inside this hook is good farming land following along the sea for several miles.

At this point there is a plateau, and on this plateau Joseph Marie Roy dit Desjardins, about 1770, established his home. His wife was Marianne Michaud. They had five sons: Joseph, nicknamed Jose, Ignace, Antoine, Olivier and Edouard, and four daughters. The daughters married and went to live in surrounding localities.

The sons all established themselves at Dry Point, each one raising a family, so in time the village numbered about one hundred people, including servants, etc. So Dry Point was the birthplace of the Roy dit Desjardins family. The genealogy of the family seems to show that Antoine Roy came to Canada from the small town of Sens, near Paris, France, in 1667. He married in Quebec on September 11th, 1668, Marie Major. In the one hundred years following, the descendants of this family separated into two branches: one became known as the Roy dit Desjardins, and the other as Roy dit Lauzier. There is no record giving a reason for this. The Desjardins, one of the branches, were located at Dry Point.

In the year 1857, or about that time, the great grandfather, Joseph Marie Roy dit Desjardins, died aged 99 years.

The five sons were all established there then; they had fine homes, colonial style of houses, some large and very well built, revealing a period of prosperity in the place. All of them were built before my time, but I have seen them. All were in good condition when I was a boy.

In the period from 1800 to 1850 there was much commerce on the St. Lawrence, there being no railroad at that time, so the small freighters by sea had much to do, and the fishing was good in sardine, herring, eels, tommy cod, sturgeon and salmon; also porpoises, very large white sea animals or small whales, which are not good for food but valuable for oil and hides. The farming was good; there were many orchards, and beautiful fruit and flower gardens. Everything showed prosperity and happiness in that small community. Travelers admired the beauty of that place and the sea; the mountains, though twenty-five miles distant to the north, were beautiful to look at. There were many islands, Grose Island, Pilgrim Islands, and others, situated so they gave protection to the ships in storms.

Granduncle Ignace had built a wharf that extended a few hundred feet out in the sea with a large warehouse on it, and schooners came at high tide and moored to it. On the sea front or in the bay there were many ships or schooners, as the ships of that locality and period were all sailing vessels; not large ones, but pretty little ships. Ignace was getting old then, but still owned a schooner, and his two sons each had one; Antoine's son, Xavier, owned one, and my father and his brother each owned one. Uncle Joseph's was "La Grosse Providence," and that of my father was "La Petite Providence." All were busy men; they built and sold ships and built others.

Just a short distance from Dry Point there was a pretty waterfall pouring over the edge of a rocky hill. The falls were about 100 feet, and above the falls there was a lovely timber grove - quite a forest in extent. An Englishman named Campbell had built a home there on the brow of the hill. It was a large English rural style of mansion - a very fine building, and its situation overlooking the sea was beautiful. He had roads built in the forest; in a cleared place on the side of the hill he set out an orchard, and a large fruit and flower garden. In the months of June, July, and August the shrubs and flowers perfumed the air, which, with the fragrance and the murmuring pines made it a place fit for a king.

Mr. Campbell was not a man of leisure, but an active businessman. He had built a grist mill, a stone building three stories high. The machinery of it was run by waterpower from the fall of a large overshot water wheel, about 40 feet in diameter. It was a very large wheel; it had to be, because there was not a great quantity of water. He also erected a number of other buildings, a large warehouse or factory, and a mold loft, six or seven dwelling houses for the men employed and the management, also a wharf out to sea that was called "Le grand quai," for it was quite long, nearly a third of a mile from the shore to the end.

In addition to this wharf, for the accommodation of large vessels from England, he built a pier about two miles out from the shore. The large ships moored there, and small tenders were used to bring freight or passengers to shore.

When Mr. Campbell had finished these developments and constructions, which were on a grand scale and really beautiful, he went to England to get his lovely bride for the completion of this dream of happiness. He must have had in mind that she would faint at his feet, like Lalla Rookh with her prince, but she was not so impressed. She said that nothing he had there compared with what they had in England; that her father's stables were finer than the chateau that he had built here. She would not stay and returned to England. Mr. Campbell's great dreams of love and happiness were destroyed. In time he too went back to England, and this beautiful place remained in idleness for many years. It afterward became the property of some of the heirs. They made use of it by spending a few months there in the summer, but it was eventually abandoned. Only the chateau remains today.

The stable was a fine two-story building, large enough for a dozen horses and carriages, with rooms for the caretaker, etc. Some years later a man named Rousseau operated a clock factory in it. They built grandfather clocks, with the wheels and movement made of wood; then metal clocks came in the market and Mr. Rousseau's clock business failed.

The grist mill continued to grind for a few years, the houses were occupied by the relatives' families of the custodian in charge, Mr. Pelletier, who lived in one of the houses, his father and mother in another, and a brother and friends in the rest of them. Later on, the whole place became vacant, and finally fell into complete idleness and decay.

While the establishment was not a part of the Dry Point village, it was adjoining it and its history is the same; they grew together, and both are gone in the same way.

Chapter 2

Building Ships at Point Sec

About 1865 the railroad was built from Quebec down to Rivière-du-Loup. This took much of the business from the sea freighters. Then a steamer line was established, carrying freight and passengers to all places of importance along the St. Lawrence. This, of course, completely ruined the sailors' business and put them out of business.

My father was an enterprising man. He would not quit and built a ship large enough to sail the high seas.

It was at this time that I was put to work helping my father. It seems that I was very useful, though but 10 years old, for they kept me out of school. In those days that was not thought so important, and anyhow, I liked the work better. I hated going to school; the teacher was a severe person, and I did not like her scolding me.

The work I did was to wait on the men, and they kept me busy. I was so small I could slip between the framing timbers, a space of about eight inches, which the men could not do, run on a narrow plank, scaffold, and do all the things they required me to do. Once I fell off the scaffold, a distance of about twenty feet. I was stunned and stayed there for some time. No one had seen me fall, the men had gone to lunch, and I was left there until I recovered consciousness. I was quite dazed but able to go in to get something to eat. The men were through lunch when I came in, but I felt better, and was hungry. I ate my lunch and went to work, saying nothing about it for fear of being scolded. I did more than a man's work by getting around in the way that I could on account of my size. My brother Ted was two years older, but the men wanted me, they praised me and made me conceited. That caused me more trouble than it did good.

One day I tried to use the broad ax as the men did. It slipped and hit me on the knee, cutting quite deep, very close to the knee cap. I saw that it was serious, and fearing that I would be punished, I ran to a house away from home. The lady there was Mrs. Thomas Pelletier, the custodian of the Campbell estate. She was a good woman and fixed me so well that I said nothing at home about the accident. They had no need of me on the work at that time and I was going to school. More than a week had passed when Mrs. Pelletier asked some of the family how I was getting along; they knew nothing of it; my leg was a little stiff, but I said I had a sore knee, and I was left alone. When they heard about it the whole family were waiting for me as I came from school, and I was kept out of school and from running around for some time after that, fearing I would have a stiff knee. It turned out all right, and I was more careful with the broad ax after that.

Ship building was all done by hand work in those days. The logs were hewn in the forest, hauled down to the works, then placed on high trestles and ripped into planks with a whip saw, one man atop of the log and one below. Three or four sets of these men were kept whipping at these logs ten or twelve hours a day and made all the lumber needed. The ribs, of course, are hewn in the forest, selected from crooked trees and roots. In the construction of a ship there are no straight pieces. It is a big job to get these pieces from the trees; a pattern had to be made and a tree found that would fit it. When the boarding - which is four or five inches thick - was put on, it was first put in a steam box and made soft with steam; then it was quickly applied to the ribs by means of tackles and lever, then pinned to the ribs with wooden pins. These pins are driven tight and clear through the boarding; and the ribs then wedged. When the boarding is dried out the joints are caulked and made watertight. Everything has to be well made about a ship and it must be very strong to withstand the storms.

The beauty of the ship too is of great importance, its sailing qualities and speed. There was great competition among ship builders to produce the fastest ships.

About that time, or a few years before 1850, was a period of great development in sailing vessels. The gold discovery in California caused a rush of people to the West. The difficulty of getting there overland was great because of the slow travel by ox trains which took several months, the hardships, and hostile Indians. In the summer of 1847, it was estimated that the Indians had killed 47, destroyed 330 wagons and stolen 6,500 head of cattle. This made people choose to go by water by sailing ships around Cape Horn.

Ship building was a great business then as it is today, but very different. The first real sea-going ships we read about were developed in England. In 1607 an English company was organized to build ships for the East Indies trade. These ships were very large and very ornate palaces on the water but slow and awkward in storms. The Americans developed the first real smart sea-going ships. In the gold rush to California, 1850 and a few years following, the Americans put in commission more than 150 of the wonderful clipper ships, beautifully designed, with long and graceful lines, and marvelously rigged, acres of canvas, ingeniously arranged to stand the storms, and developing a speed nearly equal to the steam ships of this day.

Returning to the work on my father's ship: when it was launched and slid into the water I was on board, and I never was more thrilled in my life when this big thing, upon which I had been working for nearly three years, started to slide down to the water like a huge fish. Everyone there felt as I did, but our joy was short for the tide had not come in as high as was expected and she touched bottom and stopped before she floated. That was an ill omen, as it turned out, a few years later.

The next night the tide was some higher, and she floated away. In the morning I saw her there at anchor. There were no masts on her yet, and no load in her so she floated like an eggshell, high on the water and long. She looked very pretty. I can see her in my mind to this day. They named her Amelia. They towed her away to Quebec, and there she was rigged; then she sailed to all parts of the Atlantic for five years doing service between Canada and the United States, South America and Europe.

It was September before all was made ready to leave on a cruising trip that kept them away until the following September before returning home. Father went as captain of his own ship, and with him his second son, David, who was then but 17 years old. Arsene, the elder son, was left home to take care of the farm, and Ted and I were boys going to school. Whenever they stopped in ports Father would write and tell us what happened at sea, etc.

Once in the crossing from Liverpool to Baltimore they were in a bad storm and were nearly lost. Part of the rigging was torn away, the bowsprit broken, and the ship was otherwise badly crippled. It must have been very rough. Anyone who knows anything about the ocean marvels that vessels can withstand these great storms at sea - waves 50 to 100 feet high, raging along in all kinds of billows, great rolls of white foam striking the ship and passing entirely over it, washing everything off that is not securely fastened on board. When the ship rides one of these high waves next to it is a depression, a hole, just as deep as the wave is high; the prow of the ship tips and slides down to the bottom of it, poking into the next wave, sinks into it, and struggles to come to the surface again. And think of that in the night when it is so dark one can't see his own hand in front of his face, when the waves strike the ship from the side and it rolls over as if it would tip clear over! To see these angry waves in the daytime is bad enough, and a test of men's courage.

My father was used to it, having been in several wrecks before, but on landing at Baltimore on this trip his brother-in-law who was with him on this voyage left them, and never again would go to sea or on board any ship.

The next year my other brothers, Arsene and Theodore, were taken aboard, I being left alone to take care of the farm, which I understood well. Although very young, I did the work of a man.

During the next two or three years my father and the three sons continued their cruising of the high seas. When returning home, they would tell us about the wonderful things and the odd people they saw in the strange countries they visited, for they went not only to Europe but to Africa, South America, Mexico and all the islands of the East Indies.

The following year, Father had new masts put in the ship and let my two brothers, David and Arsene, navigate her while he stayed at home for a rest. Theodore was somewhat contrary and would not stay if Father was not there. Being a good sailor then, he found a job on another ship - a circumstance that shows what part fate plays in a man's life, for, a month later, our ship was lost and all on board.

Before sailing on this, her last voyage, my brothers were home for a short visit. The ship was riding at anchor in the channel, about six miles from shore. They had aboard the old masts which had been replaced by new ones, and I went with Father to tow them ashore. That was at night. We left the ship with a little breeze, and in a short time we reached shore. We moored the spars to some fastenings there and started to tack against the wind to bring the yacht to the pier, about two miles away. The wind increased and the tides were against us and we could not make it. We took down our sails, and by getting very close to shore we rowed ourselves into the lee of the pier.

The yacht had to be returned so those that were ashore would embark early in the morning. This had taken us from six o'clock in the evening until four o'clock in the morning, and I was very tired; as soon as I reached home, I fell asleep; when I awakened a while later, my brothers and the rest of the crew had left without my seeing them. I remember well the last sight I had of them; sailing with a strong breeze, they quickly disappeared back of Pilgrim Island, and I never saw them again. They never returned. My heart was so full of regret for not having stayed up and seen them leave that I could not keep from crying.

I hid myself so I could cry without being seen.

The storm in which my brothers perished was the worst ever known there. The wind was so strong that a tidal wave drove some of the ships more than a mile inland, and some others on rocks 100 feet above the sea level. Buildings were blown down, trees torn down, and much damage done.

My brothers left St. Pierre, Newfoundland, a colony belonging to France, reserved in the settlement of Canada with England as a fishing region. There is a good harbor at St. Pierre. The entrance is very narrow with hills surrounding. It was reported that when they sailed away there was so little wind that they could barely steer through the entrance, with all sails on. The wind started as they passed out of the harbor. It increased so fast and unexpectedly, and being favorable they undoubtedly kept all sails on to make time, they probably were not able to take them down for the wind got so strong that men could not stand up to it; they had to hang tight or be blown away. It is probable that the ship, going before the wind, was pushed with such force that she nosed into the water. They were going with a ballast only; possibly this ballast slipped to the fore, and the ship went down to the bottom in an instant. It is to be hoped that is the way it occurred, instead of the ship lying on its side with the raging seas beating on her until everyone was washed away. Thinking of the agony one would endure in such a case - his own life, and his own parents, his wife and children, and all that is dear to man - it was surely terrible.

We looked for some news or some reports from them for a long time in the hope that some of them survived and had been picked up by other vessels, or that some part of the wreckage had been seen, but we never have had a sign of them. They disappeared as if swallowed by the sea.

Chapter 3

The Desjardins of Point Sec

This was very sad for all of us, and terrible for my father. The loss of his sons and his property was a cruel fate. Arsene was his first child, a fine man, well-liked by everybody. David was somewhat of a genius; at 22 years of age he was a certified sea captain, and Father idolized him; he expected a great future for him; and David too, was so devoted to Father; they were pals and would spend all their leisure time together, talking of future enterprises and business; or they would be playing checkers. When this great sorrow was brought to him it was thought that it would kill him; but sorrows never kill, it is said, and this proved it - he lived for forty years after that. He eventually died of a stroke.

Father had many sad adventures in his life. He married young, and being strong and full of ambition, he started very early to build and sail ships. He had been in several wrecks. Once they were caught in a great ice floe, while crossing the Strait of Belle Isle. The ice crushed the vessel, and it sank. They were left on the ice for six days, drifting to the ocean about the great banks of Newfoundland. They were picked up by a passing vessel, just as the wind started shaking the ice, and they would all have been lost in a few hours if this vessel had not seen them. In fact, they had seen other vessels pass who either did not see them or would not give them assistance.

At another time they were shipwrecked on the Island of Anticosti. It was late in the fall, and they were compelled to pass the winter there. The winters are very severe on this island, the only occupants of it in winter being bears and other wild animals. It is a large island, 150 miles long and about 40 miles wide, and all it is good for is a home for wild beasts. The entire area is rock or marshes. The only human inhabitants are the lighthouse keepers; they are brought there in the spring and returned to the mainland at the close of the season in the fall. In later years it was sold by the Quebec Government to Menier of chocolate fame, who bought it for a hunting preserve.

Father and his crew built some quarters to protect themselves from the cold and the bears. These animals are very dangerous, and no one dared venture where they were. In the spring the shipwrecked party was brought up to the mainland and finally arrived home after being lost for seven months.

During this time my mother lived in great anxiety. She could not believe that my father was dead, although she was about to give up hope when he returned. She was so surprised when he came in that she fainted in his arms.

Later, my mother died when he was on one of his voyages. On returning home, my father found that his wife had been buried and his home was in the care of others. A maid was in charge of the house, with the older children, five of them, in her care, while the two youngest, my brother Theodore and myself, were being taken care of by others. Theodore was at Uncle Edward's, and I at Uncle Antoine's (granduncles). We did not stay there very long; my father was too proud to have anyone take care of his children, so we were brought home.

The maid that was taking care of us, whose name was Delphine Chouinard, stayed with us two or three years, until Father married again. She too married, and a few years later when I was old enough to notice and remember, she visited us, and I heard her tell my stepmother that she had been wanting Father to let her have me, and he refused. She said it nearly broke her heart, because she loved me so much. I have always remembered that; I cherish it yet because it is the only expression I have ever had, that anyone ever loved me, outside of my own babies. I know that my babies loved me, for I loved them dearly, and babies are honest and never ungrateful. It is only after they grow older that they sometimes forget.

After we had moved away from Dry Point, Father put in his time on finishing our house on the farm. This farm had been his father's property; some years previous to this time, my grandfather was drowned with two of his sons. He had a small sloop that he navigated between the islands. While out on a trip they were caught in a storm and lost.

Grandfather Joseph or Jose had married twice; in his first family, of which my father was one, there were two other sons, Uncle Joseph or Jos, and Uncle Thomas. My father's name was David. There were two daughters, Aunt Adelaide and Aunt Zoe. In the second family there were nine children, five sons and four daughters. I mention them, because I want to tell something about them later.

Uncle Jos had moved away from Dry Point, and so did Uncle Thomas, so there were no more of Jose's family left there. At Dry Point times were getting pretty bad; there was no business there anymore, since the establishment of the steamer coastal company. Because of its speed and novelty, it took all the freight and passengers. The sailors were fast enough when there was wind to push them along, but on the St. Lawrence in the months of June, July and August it is usually very calm; there were sometimes weeks during which sailing vessels would not move, and of course that was the very best for the steamers. It was so nice to ride on them, the boat going so smoothly through the water, the landscape beautiful to look at, it seemed as if the land were passing by.

Granduncle Ignace, who had done more than anyone else in the building of Dry Point, was very old then, but still working in his shop. He must have been a cooper by trade, for he was still making small tubs sold for butter containers. He was very expert at it. These tubs were made of white spruce, with hoop of white ash. They were so well made, and white and clean, there was a great demand for them. He had big logs brought to him, then sawed them in short pieces, just the length of the staves, and split them, and later when they were dry, he would shape them with a draw knife. He made the hoops also.

I was more intimate with him than with any of the other relatives. I often spent hours sitting in his shop watching him work. His shop was in the warehouse on the wharf. At times the warehouse was full of these tubs, but he never stopped working. The warehouse was a good building, and the wharf was also of good construction. He had built it when a young man; and his house was about the best dwelling at Dry Point. A good style of architecture, with a fine veranda in front, and a very ornate doorway they called the Portique. It had broad eaves with a cove underneath and ornamented frieze, and five dormer windows in the roof. In fact, that kind of a house would grace any city today.

The interior was arranged for two families. He and his wife, Aunt Justine, were living in one part, and his son Theophile with his family lived in the other part.

Theophile never prospered very much; he enjoyed his own comfort and having a good time more than work. His wife was a beautiful woman, very tall and athletic, able to handle any man. Once when Theophile and another man, because of having had too much gin, were fighting in the house, she threw them both out. When they landed at the bottom of the stairs, they sobered up and stayed out until her temper calmed down. Her name was Sophie. She came from the North, Maury Bay. They had five children, three boys and two daughters.

One day Sophie took passage with a fellow who had a small yacht, to go to her parents at Maury Bay. She took three of the children with her, a boy and the two girls. In the crossing, and close to the north shore, their yacht capsized, and all were drowned but Sophie who swam to shore in some way. The owner of the yacht and her three children were drowned. Sometime afterwards, that family moved from Dry Point to the States. About that time the grandfather died, and his beautiful house left vacant, went to ruins.

The name of the other son was David, the same name as my father, but a cousin, of course. He was nicknamed David Faiyot. He was a different type of character from Theophile - a vain sort of fellow, pompous in manner and dress, wore most stylish clothes, and had fine horses and sleighs. In winter they would go to church on Sunday with bells on the horses and ribbons on the robes, and he and his wife dressed in beautiful furs. They had no visible means of making money, so there must have been some talent there for them to carry on as they did and put it through. About the time his father died, they sold their house and removed to Rivière-du-Loup.

The third brother was Ignace. He had inherited the farm, and of course paying rent to his father. He had a large family, mostly girls, and they soon left for the States where they could find employment. One of the boys stayed on the farm, but then that branch of the family was gone from Dry Point.

Uncle Edward had been a merchant there and had retired with some money. He had four children and wanted all of them to be religious; one son was a priest and two of the daughters were nuns. One daughter married the most polite man in the country, but the most lacking in business ability. They all moved to St. Andre so as to be near the church where they could go to mass every morning.

Uncle Antoine stayed longer and was the last to leave. He was the most amiable man of them all, a fine looking, large man, and a very interesting talker. I enjoyed listening to him more than any man I ever knew. He had many fights with the Indians in the early days. He could tell of these experiences well. He was so strong that when he caught one of them, they could not get away. A big chief jumped on him once, he told us, saying, "I pushed him against the wall and got hold of both his wrists, and squirm as he would, he could not get away, and begged to be let loose, promising to be good."

He educated his oldest son Joseph to be a priest, but Joseph did not like it and went to teaching school instead. Another son, Xavier, was a failure as a sailor, then removed with his family to the States. The other son George went to be a sailor on a big English ship and was drowned. One daughter married La Plant. They had but one child; they made a priest of him, and he went away as a missionary in South America. There, going in swimming with a friend one day, a shark got him. His friend saw him go but could not help him.

Uncle Antoine was a very religious man. He believed that to be a priest was the greatest thing a man could do. His own sons would not enter the priesthood, so he raised a boy from another family and had him educated. He became a priest, and Uncle Antoine finished his days while staying at his house.

The other son of the original family whose name was Olivier was a pilot on the St. Lawrence. He married a Miss Michaud. He was drowned. His widow married again, to Edward Ennis. They had a home at Dry Point, but all are gone.
In my grandfather's family Uncle Jos was the most noted one of that time. He had a striking personality, a big man, weighing nearly 300 lbs., very active, and said to be the strongest man in

the country. They said he could lift 1000 lbs. easily. His feats of strength were never equaled by anyone else known. He was a busy and amiable man, traveled extensively, and had many experiences.

Uncle Jos was proud of his son Florian, and once sent him out on a voyage as captain in charge of the ship. When in St. Johns, Newfoundland, Florian had a sweetheart there, and married her, and of course spent more money than he should. He brought his bride home, and when he presented her, his father was surprised and offended. The girl was really beautiful, a figure like a Venus, with a pearly complexion, red cheeks, lovely blue eyes, and real golden hair. His father could not forgive him and sent him out to get a job wherever he could and kept the young wife in his family. He himself left for a long voyage and was gone about a year, and Florian got a job on a large English freighter and also returned in about a year. By that time the father's feelings had moderated, or he had forgotten his displeasure, and everything was made up. They sailed together two or three years after that, when the father's life was sadly ended by his being washed overboard and lost in a storm at sea somewhere near the Bermudas. His two sons, Florian and Philip, were with him. The storm was very bad and had partly wrecked the ship, but they managed to bring her to port. They did not feel able to carry on without their father. They sold the ship and gave up the sea. The family moved to Lewiston, Maine; some of them are there yet.

Having related the experiences of my father in previous chapters, I wish now to mention Uncle Thomas, Jose's third son, another powerful man, large and active. He had been in the lumber camps in Michigan, sailed the seas for some years, then established himself on a farm, where he died by accident. While chopping in the woods a tree fell on him and killed him. I loved him dearly and felt very sorry when I heard of his death in this manner. Cruel fate still pursuing this family, ten of them drowned at sea, and the sad ending of these good men.

So, the village has dwindled down and down, until there is but one house left. The whole surrounding country is owned by one man, a farmer, and that is all that is left of all these nice homes. The wharves, the chateau of the Campbell estate is still there, but in ruins, the grist mill is a pile of rocks; only the waterfalls are there; le grand quai is a pile of rock stretching out half a mile into the sea and can be seen only when the tide is out.

In times of prosperity, it was a happy community. They enjoyed the winters because there was very little done. Business, like Nature, slept in winter, which season was very cold and continued so for about four months. During that time there were amusements: parties, dances, and games. Everyone was comfortable, going to church Sundays and Fête Days, and everyone must attend; that's a part of the creed.

Dry Point had no church. The nearest church was the Parish of St. Andre on one side, five miles away; on the other side was Kamouraska, six miles away, and the division line was in the center of the village, so one-half went to one church, and the rest to the other. It was a great hardship on them in winter storms, but they never failed to go. The people were given services when they could pay for them. The priesthood in Canada has to be well paid. If the community is too small to support one in good style, religion is not brought to them, they must go where it is, and they do. They are happy to do it, such is their piety and training.

In the summer it is a joy; the church is the place where all meet their friends and visit, before and after mass. They make it a social occasion. Political speech-making, etc.; in election times candidates stand there before the whole congregation and debate on the questions of the day, which the people enjoy.

The sea is another source of enjoyment, when the weather is calm, which it usually is in July and August; there is boating, rowing, and singing, which is heard for miles. It is very musical to hear the voices over the water from miles away.

Dry Point is now unknown to those who pass by; the melodious ripple of the waves, the rainbows in the falls, the balmy air from the pine-covered hill are all there - unnoticed by the stranger, though not forgotten by those whose affections will not die. The place is deserted; its inhabitants, or their descendants, are scattered over America; many of the families are located in the States of Maine, Massachusetts and Vermont, some in Western Canada, but the greater number of them are in the United States. In Chicago and St. Louis are several families; others are in Denver, Seattle, and California. They have lost their identity as Dry Pointers and become Americanized.

Chapter 4

Grandfather's Second Family

As previously stated, there were nine children in the second family of Grandfather Joseph. Julius, the oldest son, left home when a young man. He located in Burlington, Vermont, and became a prosperous contractor there. He died there many years later.

The second son was Alfred, later known as Sir Charles Alfred Roy Desjardins, Member of Parliament at Quebec. Alfred was a very successful man; he had a rare personality, was very amiable, and possessed a clearness of judgment that carried him through life to really brilliant achievements. He started by building machinery on a small scale. He was successful in that and became a well-known manufacturer. When still a young man, noticing that politics were not right, the government being in bad hands, when election time came, he went to the primaries and offered to run for office, but the machine was there and refused him. His judgment told him that the people needed someone else and were ready for a change. He presented himself as an independent candidate for the people. He was elected and became one of the leaders in the affairs of the government of his country. His manufacturing establishment became larger and larger, until he employed several hundred men, and of course became rich.

He retained his place in the government for many years but went down with the Laurier Party. Laurier, due to English domination, is the only French Canadian that ever had the honor of being Premier of Canada, a man of remarkable capacity and intelligence, it was by his dominating personality that he succeeded to combat the opposition.

When he advocated reciprocity as being equally good for the United States and Canada alike, Washington agreed to it, but England opposed it, and the government fell. New elections were called, and Laurier was defeated. Laurier was French and a Catholic. The population in Canada is about one-fifth French to four-fifths of other nationalities. Immigration into Canada has always been wide open, and the great increase in the last generation has been of all nations until the population has more than doubled in that length of time. The French have not increased in number, and it was an easy matter for England to defeat Canada for its own gain; they had no scruples about doing so. Religion too had something to do with it. The world in general is getting to be more and more tolerant, but not yet so with England. Laurier favored reciprocity, and it was claimed that he also favored annexation of Lower French Canada to the United States a very logical and beneficial thing for them, and the United States would have gained by having the St. Lawrence from New York State to the Atlantic as a boundary line, which I hope will take place someday.

Sir Charles Alfred Desjardins went down with the Laurier Government; his party never came into power again, and he drifted out of politics entirely, and attended to his own business.

In the village of St. Andrew where he lived and had built his factory, he made many improvements; had a water works system put in, established a bank, built a wharf so the steamers could stop there, built a convent for the Sisters and a School for Girls as well as a Home for the Aged, run by the Sisters, and other civic improvements of great benefit to the people.

This made him beloved of everyone. He lived well and wanted others to enjoy the same. He was a lover of fine horses and had some fine ones. Only a small boy when his father perished, as stated before, he had received no education, but educated himself and became known as possessing great knowledge in the arts, literature and mechanics. He had married a Miss Dumond, daughter of one of the best-known residents there. They had six children, one son and five daughters. All were educated at the best schools in Quebec. His son was a fine organist, and played the organ at the church, and himself one of the singers. His home was open to all comers and enjoyed by all those that came. They had a very happy life; this through the efforts of this remarkable, intelligent, unassisted boy who became the greatest among them.

Chapter 5

Life at Point Sec

Having related the history of Point Sec, and that of some of my near relatives, I now wish to recount some of the personal experiences that I had at home.

Many of our family had perished by the sea, yet I loved the sea, as related before. I loved it more than anything on earth. It is in the blood, they say, and I believe it. I was raised so near the water and was so much in boats of all kinds and shapes, from the time I could take care of myself until I grew up to manhood, that I understood them, and the wind and the roar of the sea had no terrors for me.

With some of the boys in the neighborhood, we would sail out to sea and cruise among the big clipper ships. It was fine to see them come - great big things, scooting along so fast, and acting as if they were living things. I loved to see them and hoped that someday I would be sailing on one of them. They were so pretty it seemed to me as if anyone aboard must be happy; but of course, I know now that everything is not what it seems to be.

We sailed to the island and gathered the sea gulls' eggs. One time we had gone too far, and the wind came up strong against us. All night long we tacked close in to shore, but we could not buck the tide, and we landed a few miles from home. The wind had increased so it was a regular squall, and the folks at home thought we were lost. But we all returned to get a good scolding and were made to promise not to do it again.

We had traps to catch porpoises. In the ocean there are what they call porpoises; they are small dark animals, not any longer than five or six feet; but those in the St. Lawrence are fifteen to twenty feet long; they are small whales, white as snow. When they came inside the trap at high tide, with the tide going down, they did not know how to get out, so we would run them down with our barges built for that purpose.

These were built like the Indian canoe, only not so frail, made wider, and operated with oars instead of paddles. With four men at the oars, we went pretty fast, but not as fast as our game, and to get them we had to trick them.

The traps were about two miles in length and made in the shape of a crescent, and the ends turned in like the letter C. They were made of tall willows, 15 to 20 feet high. These willows were set a foot apart. To the porpoise it appeared as a fence. He could have gone through it as easily as a cow can get through a field of wheat. He didn't know that and was afraid of it. His idea was to swim to the end to get away, but there was no end to it; when he got to the end that was turned so as to send him back to the center, and he would repeat his run.

To catch the porpoise was to take a short cut and meet him at a certain point. That was a calculation somewhat like sending a torpedo to blow up a ship, only we did not have fixed rules. We made a good guess, that's all.

When we got them we had great thrills over it. We were usually six men in the barge, four at the oars, one to steer, and one harpooner. Of all the sports I know of, this is the greatest.

Then there was the eel season. Everybody knows about eels, but everybody has not seen them in their own element, that is, when they travel to spawn. It seems they come down from the fresh water to the sea. In the fall of the year, they come in great quantity; they don't like to get out of the water, but when they get to the sea, and are feeding in the grasses along the shore, the tide goes down and leaves them behind - *for time and tide wait for nobody.*

The season when they come down is very short, lasting only three or four days. We watched for them, tramping on the sea weeds and grasses where they hide, for the tide being twice a day the shores have not time to drain very much; water remains in pools a few inches deep where seaweed floats. By tramping on them, if an eel is there he darts out, then we kill him. One has to be quick for they move swiftly.

It is great sport to see these big, snakelike, black, shiny, lively things, four or five feet long. They slip between one's feet like a flash; if there is enough water, they are gone in the twinkle of an eye. You must hit them hard and stun them, then hook them quickly, for if they come to life again you can't hold them; they slip out of one's hand well, *like an eel.*

And the sturgeons - big fellows, some of them six or seven feet long, the ugliest thing you can see, great scaly back and sides, but the finest fish meat to eat that comes out of the water, or any other kind of meat. It is fine sport to wrestle with one of them. In England at one time they called it the Royal Fish because its flesh was so good to eat, and kings were fed on it. Perhaps they are yet.

Reminiscing about sports: Once I had some sport with a bull we had on the place. I had gone out to get the cows at milking time. The bull came after me. I was not afraid of him, I had scared him before, and thought of doing it again. He pounced on me like a cat. I jumped back as quick, but my heels caught in a rise in the ground and I fell backward. I put my arm out, and as I was about up on my feet again, he gave me a swipe with his horns which knocked me down flat on my back, and he rammed me down with his head. Then I grabbed his horns, so he could not gore me, and held on tight. I had one arm below the horns and the other above the horns so I could twist his neck. It was luck that I got hold of him that way. In twisting, I braced myself by putting my foot against his throat, and pushed with all the strength I had, and without knowing what I was doing, I choked him and he fell flat on his side. My sister saw me and called for help. I held on, partly under him, with a half Nelson on him so he could not get up. The two men who came to my rescue succeeded in roping his legs, and we let him go. The ropes were put on him very taut. It rained during the night, the ropes cut his legs, blood poison set in, and a few days later he was dead. Fate had decreed that one was to die. It came near to being myself.

There was a mountain not far from our house; it was quite high, hard to climb, but I liked to go up there in the summer, just so I could see far away. On top was a small plateau. There were all kinds of berries there, and flowers, and the view was beautiful. One could see for miles up and down the St. Lawrence, and all the islands, and count the ships that were passing. There were always many of them to be seen, many more than are seen today, because the smaller vessels are no more. The steamers are much larger, but there are not so many of them; they pass swiftly, so there is not so much to see. I loved to be up there when I had any leisure time; and, in fact, I often went up in my dreams.

Once I dreamed I was on that mountain, and looking over the sea. The scene changed from a sea; it was land, without trees; it seemed yellow, and as far as I could see perfectly level; all I could see was a small river. I wondered what country that could be. It seemed so broad and inviting. As I started on my way to it, I awoke. I thought of it many times it seemed so real, then it passed out of my mind. Years later in Colorado I actually saw the same scene.

Time passed quickly, I had given my time and labor for the home. I was a man now and was thinking about my own future. My brother Theodore was married and had gone to live in the States. When we lived at Dry Point there were several young men of about the same age. They were all gone now. Young Theophile, a bright fellow, had gone to the States. Philip was on board ship with his father; Antonio had settled on a farm at the Lake St. Pierre. Thomy Pelletier was in Salem, Mass., working in a shoe factory. Archibule le Vasseur was at the Lake, and Arthur was on the high seas sailing around the world.

These were all a year or two older than I. They all seemed to fare very well, and I felt lonesome at home. I decided that to linger is to lose. I spoke of leaving and Father said to me that I should stay; everything there was to be mine, etc., but I told him there was not enough for two families, and his son by his second wife, a boy then twelve or thirteen years old, would soon be a man and probably do better than I would. I had been working about ten years, and felt that I had done my duty, so I left.

My first job was to work in a furniture factory. The wages were very low, but I would learn the trade. My boss liked me, and I liked him well enough, but he was in the habit of getting on a drunk once in a while. He would urge me to do the same. I saw that was not good, and I left him. I went to my sister who was Mrs. Ennis. Ennis was a millwright and had a large establishment. I went to work with him and stayed there for a year. Then I went to Burlington, Vermont, and worked there as a carpenter for about a year. This was in 1880. There had been a panic before that, and wages were very low - $1.50 per day for eleven hours work. I was then corresponding with a cousin, Frank Michaud, in Colorado. He wanted me to come out; there was plenty of work, and carpenters were getting $3.00 per day. That looked good to me, and I decided to go West.

Chapter 6

Going West

As the head of New York Tribune, Horace Greeley advocated colonizing the west. He said: "Go west, young man, and grow up with the country."

Many went and I joined in the march, which had started twenty years before and was still going on. In 1860 it was a hazardous trip to the Rocky Mountains, but in 1880, although the country was but little advanced in development, the trip was comparatively safe. The Union Pacific Railroad had been completed across to the Pacific Coast, and other lines were under construction.

Due to the records of hardship the pioneers met with, there still existed a certain anxiety in the minds of those leaving for the west. I felt a little myself. When my mind was made up to go, I managed to get enough money together for expenses. I went to Montreal and bought my ticket to Colorado and went aboard the Grand Trunk R. R. to Chicago, then to Colorado on the Union Pacific.

At the time I left Montreal there was much snow on the ground, perhaps three feet on the level. This was on the first of April, but that was not unusual at that time of the year there.

Having very little money left, after the purchase of my transportation, I bought some sandwiches, crackers and cheese, and a few other things, and fixed myself a lunch box, which I would need on the way for there were no dining cars on trains at that time; and the sleeping cars were not in general use. It was in that year that George M. Pullman organized the Pullman Co. at Chicago for the construction of them.

The trip was really tiresome. For four days I had to sleep and eat in that seat - watching the country we traveled through in the daytime; at night it was toss from one hip to the other until daylight came which relieved me and brought me rest with the rays of the sun coming through the car-windows. The country did not interest me much, except that the snow grew less as we traveled west. Arriving in Chicago, there was but little of it and only in places, and the weather was mild.

I walked around while waiting for the Union Pacific train to be made up, and watched men transfer the baggage, being anxious that mine was coming along with me. I had a trunk for my clothes, and a large tool chest. In those days one was not considered a good mechanic if he did not have such a thing, and many tools; for everything was made by hand. The milling machinery of the present day was unknown then. Carpenters and finishers had a great assortment of tools of all kinds, and the chests were large and sometimes made fancy. The one I had was plain, but large and full of tools and it was quite heavy. While watching I saw the truck pass and my chest on top of it. The truck bumped on something and the chest slipped off and fell to the pavement. Its weight was more than it could stand. It split in two in the middle and my tools were spread all over the place. I helped pick them up, replaced the pieces of the chest in such a way we could rope it, and it was put on the baggage car for the West.

It was lucky I was there to save the pieces. They charged me 50 cents for the ropes, the last money I had except a 25-cent piece and a dime. Bt the time I arrived at Fort Collins, I had spent that whole quarter, but I still had the dime left.

We left Chicago in the evening. We crossed the Mississippi River in the night, so I did not see it. I must have been sleeping, although I do not remember sleeping very much. The next morning, we were at Council Bluffs, Iowa. There we had to wait for several hours. The depot there was new and not yet finished, and it was very cold. I went out and ran around to get warm, but it was too cold outside. There was no snow, but the temperature must have been down to near zero. The north wind was blowing strong and cutting clear through me to the bones.

I was brought up in a cold country, where there was much snow, but I had never felt the cold so much as I did here. I thought perhaps I had not eaten enough, but there was only that quarter left. I bought a sandwich and an orange. I could have eaten more but that proved to be sufficient.

A little later we left on our trip to the Rocky Mountains. We crossed the Missouri River into Nebraska. When we reached the North Platte River, that country surely looked poor. The river itself gives that impression. They call it one mile wide and one inch deep. There was not that much water in it. There had been very severe storms previous to that, and cattle suffered for water. When they found it they drank too much and perished. At one place I saw a great number of them dead by the water's edge - hundreds of them. The next morning, we were in Cheyenne, Wyoming.

Cheyenne was a very small place then. The depot was a one-story brick building, very low, and had no platform between it and the track. A space of about thirty feet was finished in gravel. The country around was dry and brown, not a tree any place; the wind was blowing hard but not so cold as I had experienced in Omaha and Council Bluffs. I took notice of the bricks in the buildings. They were a soft, sandy brick and the strong winds there, blowing the sand and gravel, had worn the corners in a round, and the mortar was nearly blown out of the joints.

I was left there, the train I came on going on to Salt Lake City and California. I waited for the little train, the Colorado Central for Denver, a new line just opened a short time before. This train made one trip a day, and left Cheyenne about noon for Denver.

On that train there were perhaps a dozen people, quite western-looking men - the way they dressed; high-heeled boots, etc. Most of them wore heavy woolen shirts, no coats, broad-brim hats, a leather belt, on which hung a gun-case and the handle of the gun sticking out a little. What those men were I did not know then; they were cattle men I learned later. The country around was all Cattle Ranches, and it was the only business there at that time.

So far, I had not seen anything very encouraging or even pleasant to look at. Of course, I was tired, I needed food, and someone to talk to. The only relief I got there was the bright sunshine and the clear blue sky.

We left Cheyenne and as we traveled south the weather soon warmed up. A few miles away from the town we came in view of the mountains, and they looked really beautiful, the lower part, which was covered with timbers, seen in the distance. A bluish atmosphere surrounded the hills and the mountain tops, covered with real white snow. This, over the smooth, level prairie of yellow dried grass, reflecting a golden glow in the warm air and the strong sunshine, made it a lovely picture.

This view revived my pretty dull spirits, and I now felt better. A little farther on at a place they called Lone Pine, where one single pine tree was growing, and which looked as if someone had planted it there (but this was not the case as tree-planting had not yet been started in Colorado), at a distance of half a mile or so from the railroad we saw a large band of antelopes, perhaps a hundred of them. Then a little farther over some deer, a dozen or so. Then I became entirely awakened, forgot that I had been tired and was anxious to get to my destination, which was Fort Collins, only a few miles farther.

Arriving at Fort Collins in mid-afternoon, I expected to find my cousin-friend at the depot. I had been corresponding with him before leaving Montreal, telling him when I expected to arrive. He was there, but I did not recognize him. I had seen him only once, thirteen years before, and he had changed in appearance, as I too had changed, for I had been only ten then. I looked for him; there were a few men on the platform, all appeared to be the same as the cattlemen I just described as having seen on the train, so I passed them by and walked away from the station. To find out where he lived, I would inquire in the village. Someone would know and tell me. On the way I saw a sign on a blacksmith shop. The name was familiar; I went in and asked if they knew my friend. The man said that he did. Then he said: "I can show you where he lives." He came out and pointed the direction of the place, and then he said: "But there is the fellow you want, coming this way." He was one of those men I had seen on the platform at the depot.

Now I recognized him by his eyes, dark eyes, and the same as his sister's that I knew well. It was very plain to me it could be no one else, yet I have never noticed any resemblance after that first meeting. They really did not have the same eyes - only the way they glanced in looking, was unmistakably the same glance. The reason he had not spoken to me on the platform was because he had taken me for a traveling salesman, he said, because I carried a satchel and was dressed the same as they dressed. He had a horse and carriage there, and we drove to his house, about three miles out from the village.

I had reached the end of my trip and was glad of it. They too were glad to have me come. When I came in the lady,

Mrs. Michaud (for my friend and cousin's name was Michaud, a relative of my father) exhibited much pleasure at my coming. They both were from the place I came from. Mr. Michaud had been in Colorado since 1859, made some money, had gone back to his native home, married, and returned here. He was now established as a successful farmer. She was pleased to have me there because I came from the home of her childhood and her own kin, the home she had left twelve years before, never to return to it. It had been a trying ordeal for her - those twelve years in the wilds of Colorado.

She had left a quiet, happy home, among good people, where crime was unknown and the neighbors interested in each other as one family, but here in the early days, without organized laws, the whole country open to the roving Indians, cowboys and riffraff of all kinds, it was different. Of course, there were good people too, but one had to be on guard, and be prepared to defend themselves, and strangers could not be trusted.

After spending the rest of the day and the evening relating my trip and giving full report of things at home, I went to bed and got the first night's sleep since I had left home.

Mr. Frank Michaud had a nephew whose name was William Michaud - living on a ranch near LaPorte. He had married a few months before and they were living in a log cabin and were going to build a new house. The next morning Mr. Michaud drove me over to their place, and I arranged to do the work for them. I started at once and continued to work without losing a day until the house was completed.

It was during the time when I was working on the house and living with them in the old log cabin, that I began to get knowledge of the country. As I got to know more about it my love for it grew more and more, and as I am writing this after fifty years of my life spent here, I still think there is no nicer place in which to live; for its air, its sunshine, and the beauty of its mountains make it as good as any place on earth, I believe.

My hope and desire to come to Colorado began when Mr. Frank Michaud had returned to his old home to get his bride, as stated before. I heard him tell then of the country, and it made an impression on me.

Mr. Frank Michaud was a handsome man and very interesting. It was told that he had made much money out there; this left me with a desire to go there when I could do so. The buffalo were to be seen there, and gold to be found. I hoped to see the country some day and perhaps live there. It became a wish in my mind, and as usual when a wish is persistent enough it often becomes a reality.

So it was that I was here. Would I stay? I did not know; only time would tell!

William Michaud had been in the country for twelve years. He came out first with his Uncle Frank, when he returned with his bride, as stated before. Arriving in Colorado, William had not found things as he expected, and had gone over to the Black Hills, South Dakota, where there was a great gold excitement at the time he lived there. He was there for a few years and later returned to Colorado, stopping at LaPorte. There he met Mrs. Orleans, a widow who owned a General Merchandise Store there, and married her. William liked farming better than selling groceries, so they traded the store for 160 acres of land under the new irrigation ditch, and enough money to build the house. This became the homestead of the family. Trees were planted in places to protect the house from the west winds that blow strong there in the early spring, and for shade; also, an orchard with all kinds of fruit-trees, etc. Twenty years later it had developed into a fine estate, with a number of fine buildings, gardens, etc. - the home that the hardworking, industrious and conscientious man deserves, and usually gets.

The place where I was building the house was about a mile from the village of La Porte. I often went there. Mr. and Mrs. Provost were very congenial and seemed to like to have me visit them. Mr. Provost would offer me a glass of beer or a cigar. I sometimes accepted, but usually would only thank him for I did not smoke then, or very rarely, and beer I cared very little for. It has always been a sort of cheap fermentation to me, more for animals than for man, and I thought really unfit for women. But in time I found out that people get used to it, and sometimes they get so strongly used to it that it becomes harmful to them in more ways than one.

Chapter 7

La Porte: The First Civilized Camp in Colorado

The hills just above La Porte are of a peculiar formation. They lie in broken short ridges of colored stone. They are called Hogbacks, among which the Cache La Poudre River flows. La Porte, as its name shows, was a French settlement, first established by the trappers on the river, the Cache La Poudre. Its location is six miles west of Fort Collins, or by the foothills and at the entrance of the pass into the Rocky Mountains. The caravans going west on the Santa Fe trails would take either the pass to the south through New Mexico, or to the north through La Porte, on to Wyoming and Oregon, or California. La Porte was the resting place; when they could afford to rest, they stopped for some time.

The Cache La Poudre River was first recorded as Patiras Creek. A trapper by that name had a cabin close by it, a little distance below the foothills. Reports from early expeditions were that it was but a creek - and others that it was a navigable river, from those who had perhaps seen it in early spring when fields from sudden snow melted and swelled it to half a mile in width sometimes. Later some other trappers had a camp on the river in the foothills. They were afraid of the Indians and must hide everything from them. One day someone saw a band of Indians coming toward them. Knowing that the Indians, seeing the powder they had, would take it away from them, this fellow ran for his life toward the camp, shouting "Cache la Poudre!" The Indians either did not see them or would not trouble them. They went by. The scare became a real joke, and for want of a name, the river was referred to as Cache la Poudre, and was eventually recognized by that name.

In 1844 Antoine Janis, a Frenchman, had located a claim on the Cache la Poudre, a mile above the site of La Porte. He had a cabin there. Later he went to Fort Laramie, but returned to his camp in 1858, with his brother, N. Janis, and another man named E. Gerry. They found about the place a settlement of the Arapahoe Indians - about 150 lodges of them. The chief asked them if they wanted to stay there, and they said that was what they wanted. Then the chief called a council of the braves, in which they decided to donate the land to the white men.

A company was formed, including the three mentioned above, and Tom Randal, Raymond B. Goodwin, John B. Provost, Oliver Monisette and A. Lebon Rovofiere. They built a number of houses or cabins for accommodation of the travelers that were going over the Cherokee Trail, for California and Oregon. They called the place Colona.

In 1863 this village of Colona was removed to La Porte, about a mile lower down on the river where there was room enough to build a larger town, which they believed it would be some day. There the La Porte townsite was filed on as a squatter's claim, 1800 acres being taken in for the purpose.

John Provost had taken a claim there and built a hotel and a store. Also, a ferry across the river, for in the springtime there was much water coming down from the snows of the Medicine

Bow Range. His charges were $10.00 for a wagon and $5.00 for a man on horseback. He had built a pier on each side of the river and used a sort of tram to pull his boat across. This is all gone now but parts of it were still there when I came west.

In 1863 a Post Office was established at La Porte, and the place gained in importance, with many of the settlers French - Antoine Labris, Alphonse La Rogue, Jas. Mesien (called Mason), Rock Bousquet (called Bush), Jas. and Phillipe Lariviere, and others.

At that time a company of U. S. Infantry came from Salt Lake, where they had been sent to quell an uprising of the Mormons, but had found nothing to do there, and were coming down over the Cherokee trail, returning to their headquarters in Kansas. They camped at La Porte and stayed there for some time. Later a cavalry post was established there - but finding that the floods caused them much trouble they moved away to higher ground, and later moved again to Camp Collins, six miles southeast, now known as Fort Collins, but there never was a fort there.

Of those who settled at La Porte, John Provost was an interesting character. He had married a squaw. When she died he married another. There were no white women in the country at that time. He had five or six children by the latter, and these when grown up stayed among the white people, but associated with the Indians as well. This woman either died or went back to the tribes. For Provost later on married a white woman, with whom he lived to a very old age. This last Mrs. Provost, a French woman of a good and well known family of Montreal, Canada, was of an adventurous disposition, and had gone to California at the time of the gold rush, traveling by sea to Panama, across the Isthmus, and to San Francisco by sea. She did not like it there and, returning by land, stopped at La Porte, and at Provost's hotel. He was not slow in offering her a home and she took him at his word. That was the best bargain he made in matrimony. She was a very bright and good woman and he lived very happily with her for the rest of his life, or until she died, and she died only a short while before he did.

I knew them both personally. Mr. Provost had been a lively man in his time, good-looking and well liked. Mrs. Provost could not be called pretty, but she made up for that in other ways. She should have been an actress; she was a good singer and seemed to know everything worth knowing, literature, plays; and as for history she was as good as an encyclopedia. La Porte was pretty busy then. It was on the main line of traffic. Travelers would linger there before starting over the pass on the Cherokee trail, for it was a hard and long pull to the Laramie plains.

The hotel gave parties and dances and they had gay times. In summer these parties were held in Provost Grove, which was a popular place for picnics.

A friend once told me: "Once we had a party there, all French, about 20 families. We had a good time - everything to eat and drink, races and games. Then Mrs. Provost suggested that the men vote on the woman with the prettiest feet. The suggestion was not well received because Mrs. Provost, though quite fleshy, had very pretty, small, hands and feet. She was not so good-looking but had a very fair complexion. The other women protested and said that would not be modest. Mrs. Provost said their protest was caused by jealousy, not modesty. This caused a discord in the party and the idea was given up. No one ever knew who had the prettiest feet."

Rock Bush was another interesting character - over six feet tall, very nice looking, light blond hair, and blue eyes, very quiet manner - a man that everybody would like. The best hunter and fisherman in the country. He could get trout out of the river when others would see none and say there were none there. Rock married an Indian woman, said to be the finest looking squaw of the Arapahoes, and they had real good-looking girls among them. I never saw her; she died before I came - but I was told she was tall, slender and had beautiful brown eyes. They had three boys who turned out to be fine men - good looking six-footers. They stayed among the whites and one of them became a prosperous cattleman. Mr. Bush married again a white woman and raised a family of several children. He died a very old man - they said 92 or 94. No one knew which was right.

Then there was Alphonse Laroque, a very large man, 6ft. 4 in. and his pal, Peter Dion, 5 ft. 4 in. They were out of proportion, one to the other, but very good friends, except when drunk. For they had such fights that people wondered how they could live and be friends afterwards, but they were.

Jos. Mason lost an arm in a battle with the Indians, but that did not prevent his being successful. Later he owned a general merchandise store in Fort Collins, also a ranch of 600 acres of fine land. The Indians tried many times to kill him, but failed. He was killed, however, by his own horse. The horse kicked him over the heart, and he died instantly. Phil Lariviere had been his pal and grieved over the accident. Then four years later he too was kicked over the heart by a horse and died in the same manner.

The following story was related to me about little Joe Slade: Joseph Slade, who was in charge of the Overland Stage, was a good man for the place but a dangerous man when drinking. In his supervision of the line he established a post on the plateau just west of the Cherokee Pass and called it Virginia Dale, in honor of his wife. He was surely a dare-devil - had always been. When a boy his father managed to send him to Texas. He grew up and married there. Then came to Wyoming and Colorado. Why the Overland Stage Co. employed him was questioned, but they thought was that the place needed a man like him to cope with the rest of the ruffians who roved the country at that time. Slade was mean and kind at times. Once he was boasting that no one dare tell him to shoot. A fellow named Farrar, who was drinking too, said: "I dare you to shoot me"; and Slade shot him instantly. Then said he was sorry for doing it, and immediately sent a messenger on a fast horse to get a doctor, who was one hundred miles away. But it was of no avail; Farrar died. Another time he had trouble with Jules Reni, another Frenchman, who had a ranch on the South Platte River. In the quarrel Reni shot Slade with a shotgun. Reni was satisfied, he had put thirteen buckshot into Slade, and said: "When he is dead put him in one of these old boxes and bury him." Slade heard him and said: "I will live long enough to cut off your ears - don't trouble yourself about my burial."

It just happened that the Superintendent of the Road was on the Stage. He ordered the arrest of Reni, and a mob proceeded to hang him. They got the rope on him and let him strangle until he was black in the face, then let him go.

But he must leave the country, which he did and did not return for some time. Slade got over his troubles to some extent, but some of the buckshot was left in his body and reminded him of his promised vengeance, and one day he sent word to Reni that he would kill him on sight. When Reni got the word, he told his friends that he was going to kill Slade. Slade heard of this and at once went to where Reni was. Not finding him he reported to the officers at Fort Laramie. They told him that his life was not safe, and Reni must be captured or there would be no peace. Slade sent some of his men to a ranch where Reni was, they captured him, and kept him in a corral near the station. Slade came; walked to the corral and as he saw Reni, on first sight leveled his gun and fired. The first ball went through Reni's mouth, but did not kill him. A second shot went through his head and he died instantly. Then Slade surrendered, but the officers had advised him to do the killing, and of course he was discharged. It was said that Slade cut off Reni's ears according to his promise.

Slade was really a bad man, peaceful enough when sober, but dangerous when drunk, and he was that way much of the time. Once he entered a grocery store at La Porte and had his fun shooting holes in the canned goods on the shelves. When he was living at Virginia Dale he often came down to La Porte. On one of these trips he went into the store again, the only one there. He smashed the mirrors, opened the faucets on the vinegar and molasses barrels, spread the flour and sugar in it on the floor to see what kind of a mixture it would make. When he sobered up, he came around and paid $800.00 for the damages. His brawls became more and more frequent, and the Vigilantes decided his fate. A rope was passed over the limb of a tree and he was made to stand on a box with the rope around his neck, and they pulled the box from under him. His wife had been called but she came too late. She cried very bitterly: "Oh, why did they not shoot him instead of hanging! If I had been here, I would have done it myself. He should not have died by the rope of the hangman." If she had been there, probably there would have been some great doings for she was good with a gun herself, and not afraid.

In 1863 a Soldiers Camp was established at La Porte, and these soldiers would accompany the stage lines and the emigrant trails, guarding them against Indians, whose depredations were bad, and also against Mexican desperadoes and stock thieves. The troops patrolled these convoys up to William Springs on the Laramie Plains and returned to La Porte. Others were detailed for the country beyond.

There were no safe places. Bandits were everywhere. They would appear as if coming out of the ground. Occasionally and in an instant a band of Indians or white marauders would swoop down on even these guarded trains and overpower or kill the men, run off with the stock and rob the people of what they had. The Overland Stage Co. had to pay for much of it, and they had to have pretty rough men in their employ to cope with that class of desperadoes.

Oftentimes some of these were men of apparent peaceful nature who would commit these offenses in the night and return to their home unnoticed. If these attacks were made in the daytime, it was pretty sure to be the Indians, but night attacks were most sure to be by white men, but no one would know who they were.

The story was told that an east-bound Overland Coach was held up near the crossing of the North Platte. The driver was killed, and the robbers carried off a small safe containing $70,000 in gold dust, which was being shipped by Express from California to New York. The robbers were never captured or found. This happened sometime in September 1862.

In the late fall a German and an Irishman came to John Provost's Hotel at La Porte with a great quantity of gold dust, claiming to have discovered a rich mine. A year later they again stopped at Provost's place on their way from the mountains, and each had six or eight thousand dollars' worth of gold dust on them - which they said they got from the mine, but they would not tell where the mine was. The next year the same Irishman was killed in a fight. The German continued to make his trips to his gold mine, returning always late in the fall with much gold dust.

Since he would not tell where the mine was, a party decided to follow him. When he passed through La Porte to go up to the Mountains, two men followed him, but he saw into their plans and changed his direction and went up into the Arapahoe Peak region. He eluded them and never was seen after that.

In 1864 a band of Indians were coming, it was said, intending to pillage the town, and Captain C. C. Hawley was not well prepared to defend the place; so he set out pieces of stove-pipe all around the walls of a corral, and made it look like cannons pointing out, thinking the Indians, taking that to be a fort, would not dare attack - if they saw it. But they never came near the place and the whole matter turned out to be a joke.

La Porte in '59 had more people than Denver, but Denver grew fast. Camp Collins was located where Fort Collins now is, and La Porte became less important. Fort Collins was to become a large city and must have more room in which to grow.

In La Porte there was not much to do in those days. People knew one another and trusted one another - and doors were never locked. The only law governing in the village was the Golden Rule - thinking of the other fellow as well as oneself was quite the custom. There was no use for law, lawyers or courts, and there weren't any. Trapping, hunting and fishing were really the only occupations. Farming was not thought of as yet - except small amount of vegetable gardening. In 1858 there wasn't a white woman at La Porte and the social manners there were of the prairie styles. Indian women would feast on dog meat and on occasion they would get a fat dog, boil it in the kettle until it was real tender (the meat tasted like young pig's and was considered very fine with corn cakes). Hoe-cakes were made of com, ground by hand on a stone. This was related to me by persons who had seen these parties and knew the Indians well.

Then farming was developed on each side of the River, and extended, in time. The idea of irrigating, which had been brought from the Mormons at Salt Lake, was put into application, and found to be good. The soil was good and wonderful crops were raised by using the water; for there was very little rain. For months there was no rain at all, and the River had plenty of water.

The Cache la Poudre was a good-sized river then. One would hardly believe it now, looking at it, since fifteen large irrigating canals have been taken from it. Below these canals the riverbed is nearly dry - except in early spring and after heavy showers. The Cache la Poudre is a pretty river. It meanders down the mountains from the snow-capped Range to the prairies for about ninety miles and falls into the South Platte thirty miles farther east. The canyon of the Poudre, as they call it, is very narrow in places and cannot be used for a pass for anything else than the waters it carries, and detours have to be made, but in other places it is really fine, and many beautiful places are now used for summer residences, hotels and parks. It is one of the nicest canyons in the Rocky Mountains.

In the early '70's a stage line from Fort Collins and La Porte went to Rustic, a pretty place in the canyon, fifty miles up the Poudre River. The Rustic Hotel there was well patronized. Many went up every day. A coach with six horses would go up at a rapid rate for 85 miles, then stop at Livermore, where lunch was served. A new relay of horses was put on and the rest of the journey made before dinner time. The stage was always loaded. At times two stages were needed. The trip was greatly enjoyed by everybody, and so was the time spent at the Rustic.

People were coming now in greater numbers and development went on rapidly. The cattle business soon became of real importance, hundreds of miles of prairies in all directions were used for this purpose. The number of cattle the country could support was unlimited, and they let the cows take care of their own calves. A herd would double in number in three years' time, so it was very profitable. Those that had money brought herds from Texas, drove them here and turned them loose.

Chapter 8

Then Came the Round-Ups

These round-ups each year were gala days and would last more than a month. There were cattle men in great numbers and the cowboys, very expert and brave men. It was better than a circus to see them in action. Their horses were trained to do wonderful things. These horses were usually small ponies, a cross between the bred horse and a Bronco, or the wild Indian pony. They were quick and very hardy and intelligent animals.

I had an experience once with one of them. My cousin said one of their cows had run off - and must be within the herd at the foothills which was about five miles away. I offered to go and get it. I had seen the cow and would recognize it by the brand. I went on the little black mare, a trained round-up cowboy pony and found the cow in a herd of five hundred or perhaps a thousand. As soon as the mare located the cow I wanted to cut out, she did the rest better than I could have myself; and then we went toward home. We came to a ditch some ten or fifteen feet wide and full of water. The cow would not jump into the water and ran along the side of it. I made the mare lope alongside until I got ahead. The cow turned and ran the other way. We repeated that several times. Then I planned to run so close to the cow that she could not turn. That proved alright, and the cow leaped into the water in the ditch. The mare started to do the same. I did not like that and said, "Whoa." She stopped so short that I slipped clear over her head, hitting on my back close to the edge of the ditch. I was stunned but able to get up, a little sore. The mare was waiting for me. The cow had crossed the ditch and was running home.

When it was discovered that irrigation would be profitable, ditches were built to take the water from the river. Companies were organized for the purpose, for it was too costly for one party alone. Water was appropriated and the whole scheme became practical and a reality.

Covered wagons were passing every day, coming from Kansas and Arkansas, going to Oregon. The cry was "Oregon for farming." These farmers wanted a change, but they did not like the dry climate of Colorado and went on by. They were a pitiful lot to see on the march - tramping in the dust of the prairies, unwashed, unshaved, and in rags, for months. The Indians were fine, good looking men alongside them. The Indian is the man of the plains. He has no beard, wears but little clothing, usually buck-skin, and appears fairly neat. His hair is very black and coarse and does not mat like the white man's hair. His skin is bronze and shines. He is straight and supple, looks healthy and seems to belong to the place.

These caravans passed through Colorado, and entered the mountains at La Porte, going north to Laramie, and on to Oregon. It is said that the hardships of the trip made new men of them. They reached Oregon and found it the promised land and became rich landowners there.

Twenty years after the great rush to California and Colorado, the covered wagon and ox-teams (the only thing that really could survive the ordeal of such a trip) were still coming every day. The result was a new generation, the Westerners or natives of the plains, who waste no thought on his neighbor's birth or the way he makes his prayer. What a man came from, or what his religion, made no difference to the Westerner. What a man himself proved to be was all that counted. Miners, farmers, cattlemen, all went as one class, as did professional men, doctors, lawyers or priests. All dressed alike and lived alike. Places of business were open every day. Sunday was no different than other days. Hotels, saloons and dance-halls were open all night. Sometimes when morning came, a party would leave the saloon for the burial grounds, and someone wouldn't return, and not much was said about it.

Once in a while new discoveries were made in mining, and new camps started. Then people would rush to them, taking themselves and all they owned, to be there first, and perhaps get squatters' claims. Sometimes it was a regular stampede - wagons where they could go with them, pack mules and burros, or on foot.

A village of a thousand or two or three thousand people would grow up in a week or two. The first to come would select the best places and sell to later comers and made money that way; and lodging houses and saloons were built in the night. The lumber merchant's wagons, and all kinds of materials, would fill the road for distribution. It was hurry, hurry, and the excitement was great - but it did not always pay. If the mines proved good it was alright, but in many cases the mines did not materialize. The camp would peter out, and the place be abandoned. A place that was built in less than a month's time, with sufficient buildings and quarters to care for three thousand people was left entirely deserted six months later, and two men were left to take care of it. I personally was in a place like this when it was being built, and saw it again six months later, with two inhabitants only.

There have been many other similar cases in the State. These excitements occurred as often as new discoveries were made, and, of course, many of them were profitable and turned out to be real good towns, and many of them are prospering today.

Gold excitement will lure anyone. It always has. In 1858 and 1859 it brought fifty thousand people to Colorado, as it would again, if new strikes were made. That may happen again any time, considering the small places that have been worked in these mountains - more than 1,000 millions taken from them it is hard to believe that no more is to be found. Some say that only a little start has been made.

And now returning to my own experiences in La Porte: The William Michaud house was finished, and the folks moved in and everything was satisfactory. I spent a little of my leisure time building a small boat. A short distance from the place there was a lake near the foot-hills, a fair sized lake, perhaps a mile in length. It would be nice to have a canoe on it, I thought. It would make it more like home, so I built one and put it in the water. I used it a few days - but leisure would not bring me anything, I thought, and so I left it there and went to Fort Collins to find work. Some hunters asked me if they could use the boat, and I let them do so. They hauled it from one lake to another, and it was used by everyone who wanted it; but I never saw it anymore. The last I heard of it, it was on the Linden Meyers Lake 10 or 15 miles from where I had left it. That was my first investment and there were no returns from it.

After finishing the boat, the next thing was to look for work somewhere else - work that would pay. That was not easy for I was much of a stranger yet. I consulted with Frank Michaud, who was really the one cause for my coming west, and, of course, my best friend. At that time the Catholics had no church building there - only a mission. A priest was appointed by the Bishop to give services in several small towns. These services were held at someone's home who was a member of the congregation, once a month or so, as this one priest alone was able to get around.

Mr. Michaud and others had decided to have a church or chapel, and they had bought a schoolhouse which had got to be too small for the town.

They wanted to transform it into a church, so Mr. Michaud put me to work on it. He arranged it so I could get the materials and I did the work. I put in a new floor, built an Altar, and a railing to separate the sanctuary from the main body of the church. The Altar was made in a very inexpensive manner. The lower part was framed and covered partly with wood, and linen draperies. The upper part was made by using a dry goods box - on end with a little round top door, neatly ornamented on the front of it on the outside and finished inside with white silk for the tabernacle. On each side of this box I built some low shelves, in a recessing way, so candle sticks could be placed on them, and on the top of the box I built a sort of a dome with a Cross on that. When the Altar was decorated in the manner in which it is usually done, it looked very well, and did not cost much. As I remember, it cost about twelve dollars. The priest, whose name was Father Cummings, said that in the eyes of God it was as good as if it cost that many thousands.

In the body of the church I built some pews, 32 of them, so the seating was a little over 100. In the rear I built a small loft or gallery. Someone donated a small organ, and they had choir training, and after a while were able to have high Mass, and some fair singing. The organists were Lizzy McDougal and Ella Purcell, and nearly a dozen others as singers, including myself. I was not gifted as a singer. My voice was good enough, but I lacked time and expression, and it was that way with most all of them, with the exception of one, Miss Purcell. Without her we could not have had much of a choir. She was a real singer, a fine soprano and had most perfect time sense. She seemed to know everything about music. When all the rest were off, she would be carrying the whole load - until they came on the tune again. At times it was very hard for her to keep them on the music, but she was usually able to do it. She was really a master; her voice was very sweet and capable of expansion so as to dominate all the rest when necessary - which was often the case.

I very much admired her for her music - it is such a God-given gift to be a real good singer. Other branches of the Arts, it seems to me, are greatly mechanical, as in painting for instance. There is perhaps one in a thousand, or a million, who is a great artist - the rest are not gifted artists but copyists, which can be learned, but no one can copy a real singer and that is the reason why there are so few Tetrazzinis and Carusos. I felt a strong attraction for this girl - sure enough there were several others who were good girls and nice to me. But it was hard for me to even think on the subject of getting married for I was not sure that I could support a wife. I was then working for a contractor who had a contract on a large building in which he failed, and I lost $250.00 of my wages with him. I was living at the Windsor Hotel, the best in town. It was new and they needed tenants, so I was getting a very low rate, as a regular boarder. I managed to keep going, getting work from other parties, etc.

All this time we had our choir rehearsals and I was thinking more and more about this being alone, when one could be so happy, having a family of his own. I attended practice and church regularly, and the girls all told me that I sang very well. Ella, the good singer, said that we should practice on a nice piece. The Bishop was to be there for Confirmation and we should have something for the ascension service. I said, "alright". She selected O Sponsa Mea Delecta Venit. It was a very nice piece but hard to sing. She sang the soprano and I tenor. We finally had it so we could go through with it. It was very hard on her but not so much on me, for I depended on her entirely for time and control. We had rehearsed the Masses that we knew pretty well, so when the Bishop came, he was pleased and told us that our singing was good.

This was Bishop Machebeuf - first Bishop of Colorado - who came from France when a young priest, was sent to Santa Fe, and later to Denver, then made Bishop of the state. Bishop Machebeuf was a real pioneer and here at the time when the Indians were very bad. On one occasion he was shot by them and severely wounded. This left him with a short leg, and he limped for the rest of his life.

On this visit he stopped at the Windsor Hotel, and I was living there at the time. I offered my services to help take care of the things he had with him for use in the ceremony. He accepted and I walked to the church with him. After the ceremony we repeated the walk back to the Hotel. It was then that he thanked me and complimented me on our good singing, which was not really mine but Miss Purcell's. This made me have even more confidence in and respect for her, hearing this praise from this very good man.

Among all these girls in the congregation there was a very pretty little widow. She had lost her husband a short time before; how was she to get along now? Others said: "She can get a better man now; who will make the right kind of living for her"; and I was told they meant me. Then I thought it was good they did not know how hard up I was, but living at the Hotel was the reason for their superior opinion; which is often unreliable, and many are sadly deceived by display like that.

The widow was an accomplished lady, highly educated, a fine pianist, and had very fine manners. But she was too small physically, being very slight and very frail, and I could not think of being wed forever to so little a woman as she. Then Christmas time came, and I got little gifts for every one of my friends. I went to Ella's house with something for her, and the other children, and for her mother - I had a big cane, actual sized cane, made of candy, I said to her: "This is for you for it is said that the gift of a cane means a long life," and she was delighted with it.

Then on New Year's Eve I walked to the country, about four miles, to Mr. Michaud's place with some little gifts for them and the children, arriving there just about 12 o'clock for the New Year. They had retired for the night and were asleep. I had to make a big racket to wake them up. They finally heard me and let me in. We did not go to bed until near daylight. This was the first New Year's racket I attended in Colorado.

One Sunday after church I walked with Ella - Miss Purcell - to her house. They invited me to lunch with them. After church we went horseback riding a few miles out. After returning home we walked down to the river and sat down and played in the clean sand. With a stick I drew the plans of the house I proposed to build when I got married. She liked it. We talked about everything - then planned to have a picnic. We decided on a Sunday when there would be no priest, therefore, no church. Later when in my room I write invitations to nearly a dozen parties. I said there would be no church on that Sunday and it would be nice to have a picnic at Provost Grove at La Porte, each to bring their own lunches, there would be something to interest everybody.

They all came - the Michauds, the Labris, the Bernards, Dions, Roucalls, MacDougals, Gills, Gardners, Purcells and myself, and others. I had a case of lemons and 10 lbs of sugar, 100 lbs of ice - and as soon as we got there, I made a barrel of really good lemonade. We fixed up swings in the trees and everybody had a great time. Then the lunches were spread, and some were real lunches, fried chickens and cakes and pies, and all sorts of pretty things. When it was all set, one party wanted me at their place, and so did the others; fearing there would be some bad feelings come from it, I decided to camp with the Purcells. Miss Ella and I had planned the party and I felt I should be with her; it turned out peacefully, and everybody went home happy.

Chapter 9

Marriage

Later the little widow remarked that Ella had really poor manners, for something she did not like. It seemed to me like a little jealousy, and that caused the deciding point in my mind. Ella was so much more capable and would be a better companion for me. She was a good worker, played the organ and piano and was as fine a singer as I had ever heard. Her health seemed good - she had the rosiest cheeks I ever saw. So I decided for her. I proposed that very day. She accepted - and we agreed on the date for our wedding.

We decided to keep it quiet until the time came. I did not have money enough to make any showing, and we would have only the few of our most intimate friends attend. But the day before the wedding I went to collect some money and the party wanted me to wait for a week or so. Then I told him that I was to be married the next day and must have it. He gave it to me, but he told about the wedding. The result was that we had the little church filled with people, a big surprise for me. A friend who was reporting on the evening paper was there and gave a full report of it - so the more we tried to keep it secret, the more public it turned out to be.

If a fellow has not acquired the means of making a livelihood for himself and a family before getting married, he had better get at it very quickly, for he is now in the place where he soon will be forced to provide. The greater the man, the greater the care and responsibility he will undertake for success. The start must be made in youth. I realized that. I had been thinking about it, and wondered what destiny had in store for me. I was now 26 years of age, and my wife just over 20. We both realized that we had to work, and as we felt able to do it our hopes were strong, and we gained in experience. While on our way we managed successfully enough, and soon found ourselves with a family, and our hearts filled with the joy of having children of our own.

We had many friends too, good friends that made life dearer for us. If we have friends around us, everything around seems good - the surroundings, the air, the climate, the scenery, all appear to be good - even hard work is forgotten for the sake of friendships. It is as if Nature too wants to be our friend - the sunshine and the rain, the wonderful flowers and trees, and the birds that chirp and sing so sweetly. The little snow-birds in the cold snow, singing with joy as if happy because they are numerous. If we are not happy it must be our fault for Nature wants us to be, and like the birds we should find happiness in our everyday work, which is for our own needs, and the good Providence rewards our own efforts - and the desires of our hearts. To labor is the greatest source of joy in life - few stop to think that way perhaps, but there is a time in the life of all of us when we do, and we realize that nature in human beings is not very different from other living things.

May Eleanor Desjardins (c.1905, age 16) at the Desjardins home 1177 York St, Denver, where Bernard lived until his death. Bernard and Ella had nine children: Leo, May, Clotilde, Elise, Joseph, twins Regina and Virginia, John, and Richard
Hume Family Archives

To admire a building or any large object, one has to retire from it to a distance proportionate to the size of the object it was for this reason that people moved to the foothills and located the town of Fort Collins, where it is now several miles from the mountains, where a picturesque view is had of Long's Peak and the range running South to Pikes Peak. There the surrounding country is very good for farming and the railroad from Denver to Cheyenne passes through the town. The stone quarry is nearby, with very fine building stone and in great demand. At that time Fort Collins grew fast and was expected to become a large city. The resources, however, were not sufficient for that and the town stopped growing after it was large enough to take care of its own people and the surrounding territory. Investors, speculating on chances, saw that it would not grow much more and would not invest.

I had no knowledge of the causes that build a town. I did not even think about it. I had my home and enjoyed it there. On the rear end of my lot, which was about 200 ft deep, I planted fruit trees, forty of them, and after a few years they made me a nice little orchard. I was contracting then and had a little mill on the edge of the river run by waterpower. I built many of the buildings in Fort Collins, including the Court House. I was generally pretty busy for the few years I lived there.

Chapter 10

Return to Point Sec

When Fort Collins ceased to expand and there was little building anymore, I removed myself and my family to Denver. In Denver it was a little hard to get started, but in time I made friends and soon got very busy. I sold my Fort Collins home and built one here. The next few years were prosperous for us. The family was growing, and we had little to spare. Then I wanted to go and visit my father for I had been away from home twelve years. My wife was not well and would not go, but she said "You go alone. It costs less. I would like it better. It is too cold for me out there." This was in January, and it was severely cold that winter.

I decided to go alone. My trip was really a pleasant one. Only later on I often thought that I should not have gone alone. I could have waited until she was able to go with me. I still think a man should not gratify his own pleasure in any way without his wife sharing it with him. I was going to see my father and perhaps that was pardonable, and I had the pleasure of being some good to my sister.

Arriving in Montreal in a great blizzard, I found four or five feet of snow in the streets. I stayed there a while between trains. I thought of having something to bring up to father and going along the street, looking in the store windows, I noticed a very pretty, big chair. I went in and asked the price. "$50.00" the clerk said. It was a big price for a chair then, but it was a fine one and worth the money to me. I bought it and had them ship it to my father's home.

I then went to the on the train for the old home was 300 miles farther down the St. Lawrence River where the snow was to be still deeper. The railroads in that country, those built 75 years ago, were straight. They did not curve around to go into the villages but went by in a straight line. If the village was on the line all right, but if off the line, the road would not come to it. In this case my father's home was about 5 miles away from it.

I got a driver to take me to it. We got to the place where I was born, Dry Point, or about two miles away from the home, I said to the driver, "About here used to be a big drift that tipped nearly everyone over as they passed over it." It was dark then and we could not see. But just then we got into it and our sleigh turned clear over. I landed in deep snow 15 feet away but not hurt. Rather pleased instead. Like old times at the same old place.

Half an hour later we arrived home, and they sure were surprised to see me. The next day my half-brother went for my trunk, and I told him there would be another package. After a while, we saw him coming, and in the open sleigh we could see the trunk and a great big package. "What can that be?" they said. When he arrived, they brought the package in the house and we proceeded to open it, and lo and behold, it was the big chair. My sister said, "Quel beau fauteuil" (what a beautiful armchair). It looked fine. A red plush heavy parlor chair and everybody was excited over it. Father was standing there, not saying anything. Then I went up to him and took him by the arm and led him to the chair and bade him sit down, which he did. And then I said, "This Father, is for your comfort in your old age." He did not say anything, but tears ran down his face and my sister put her arms around my neck. She kissed me. She too was excited to the point of crying.

The house of David Desjardins at about the time of Bernard's visit
Hume Family Archives

I stayed home about a week, then went back to Montreal to visit another sister, underline, Mrs. Lamarre, living a few miles out of the city. When I arrived there, I found them in a distressed condition. Her husband had been sick for a year. He was a lawyer and had lost all his business and my sister said he had not paid the premium on his policy. I told her to give it to me and I would see if I could take care of it. When in Montreal I saw the agent and offered him the money. He took it charging me a little interest. My brother-in-law died two months later, and his wife received $2,000 which was a great help to her and a pleasure to me.

From my sister's place, I went to see my brother, Theodore, who lived in Attleboro, Massachusetts. After a few days there I left for home but went through New York City. I stayed there a while. I had never seen New York. It was a big city then, though not a quarter of the size it is now. There were no skyscrapers, no underground railroad, and only one bridge - The Brooklyn. The Columbia University had quarters in the city and was little known. Riverside Drive was a country road.

While I was there, I met with some Denver men. They were attending a meeting of the national Master Builders Association as delegates from Denver. I knew them as builders, but I did not know of this association. When back in Denver, I met them again and was invited to join them. I did. This was all I got out of my trip outside seeing my own folks, but it left me a Master Builder which gave me a little better footing in my business.

Chapter 11

The Panic of 1893

The years previous to that had been good, but then came the start of the depression that ended in a panic in 1893. I was strong and knew enough about the business to hold out and get my share of the work that went on until 1892 when there was really no work in Denver. There was an excitement at Creede where a new gold strike had been made. Some of my men wanted me to go. "You can make all kinds of money there," they said. And so, with three of them I went. At Creede, things were very rough, and no room was to be found. Mr. Lepleir, a lumber man, who I knew, offered us a tent. This was in January, and there was much snow in the hills. The tent had been set up on a pack of ice. It could not be moved for there was such a scramble for lots that none could be got. So, we slept in there with all our clothes on, except for the overcoat and boots. Creede was located along the creek. On one side was a steep cliff and on the other, there was room enough for one street, with lots on each side. So, to accommodate a few thousand people, it ran a long way up the Creek. Nearly every other door was a saloon, and the place was full of gamblers and drunks everywhere. In the night those drunks would be shooting at buildings, and someone was wounded or killed almost every night. There was no graveyard yet and the bodies were shipped like freight every day.

One night, shots went through our tent and in the morning, I discovered two bullet holes just over where I slept. That was my first day there, and it worried me some, but I got used to it for this shooting was going on very often. There wasn't so much to do there, and the excitement was cooling down for the mines were not showing as well as they had expected, and the building was about to stop. However, I found a little party who wanted to build a little store with rooms above. I made a plan and a price to build it. He accepted and we built it in a week's time I collected for it returned to Denver. The place was a fake, the mine proves of little importance. I did not like that sort of crowd anyhow. After paying off, I had only a few dollars left - so the experience was all I gained by going there.

In Denver there was nothing doing. My brother in Attleboro, Massachussetts wanted me to go and build a house for him, so I went. I left Denver for the 1st of April and by the 1st of July his house was completed, and I returned to Denver. Business was poor and building was at a standstill. I worked but little in the fall and winter, so in the spring I left Denver and went to St. Paul, Minnesota, where I expected to find my friend John Ennis. I had worked for him 15 years before and I liked him very much. He was a nice fellow and a very able man. Had large contracts there and made money. When I went there Ennis was gone. He had gone to Duluth, and I followed him there at Duluth. I found his family, but he was in Chicago. Duluth was in the middle of a panic. All work stopped, the Government was building a post office there and even that was stopped.

About 30 miles north of Duluth, in the Mountain District, a great iron mine had been discovered and they were getting ready to mine the ore and this would be on a very large scale. They had built long piers at the upper end of Lake Superior. On these a train of 20 or 30 cars would dump their entire cargo at one go, or in a minute, into bins and the Lake barges would get under these bins and load in an instant also. At the mines a city was built called Virginia City. They said there were about 5,000 people there. This may have been exaggerated. There may have been only half as many, however it was quite a place. About a week previous to my going there the place had burned down to the ground. Not a house left - two or three isolated buildings a quarter of a mile away was the only place to get anything to eat or shelter to sleep. I walked through the ruins. It was a sight - nothing left standing but a few chimneys and the foundations over the entire place of nearly a mile square, I went up to see the mines, which had been stripped and the ore exposed. Red hematite, which they scooped with steam shovels into the train cars. There are great hills of it there.

For the night I went to this isolated house, had something to eat there, and was sent upstairs with about 25 or more men. We slept on the floor on mattresses side by side. I laid down with all my clothes on - even my shoes - and kept my coat buttoned up so that if anyone should try to rob me, he would have to wake me to do it. The next morning, I boarded the train for Duluth. At Duluth the papers stated that four banks in Denver had closed their doors. That made me nervous, and I took the chain train for Chicago that night. Arriving at Chicago, I presented a draft I had on the bank, and the teller said, "Your banks in Denver are pretty shaky now, but I guess this one is alright," and he gave me the money. The next morning, the papers had it that eleven banks had closed their doors - and this included my bank. If I had not got that money the day before, I would have been stranded there. This was the start of the Panic of 1893. I visited the World's Fair for four or five days and returned to Denver.

Denver was in the worst panic imaginable. Times had been dull for some time before, but the people had little savings, but when all these banks closed down them all at once they were left with nothing to live on, and thousands had to be fed. A place was designated at Riverfront Park where it was said that 5,000, were fed for a while. This was a great crash coming down on proud the city which boasted of representing the elite society of all nations, the city that had grown from a camp of covered wagons to a metropolis in a generation. It was known all over the world. France was well represented here. The Charpiots, who ran the famous Charpiot hotel and restaurant. The Peranous, the Vidals, the Marions, and many others. England had scores of agencies pouring money into the city on speculations and interests in mines. Germany too had perhaps more of their people there than any other nation. They covered all lines of activity from the common laborer to the bankers, doctors, professors, architects, and artists. In fact, the display of talents and accomplishment was more apparent here than it was in New York City at the time. And of course, nearly all other nations were there only not so conspicuous, perhaps.

The mines of Leadville had made Colorado shine like a beacon that reached around the world and Denver was the Eden of the state. N.P. Hill and the Argo Smelters had started the boom. H.A.W. Tabor had invested his money from the mine in the Tabor Grand Opera House, the finest building of the kind in the United States at the time. Bush and others had built the New Windsor Hotel, and that too was known as the best hotel in the USA. Denver had many millionaires. It's not so important nowadays to be a millionaire, but it was then, and you had to come to a city like Denver to find them. Here were the Hills, the Moffats, the Barths, the Tabors, the Reithmans, the Kountzes and Bergers, the Hunters, the Campions, the Porters, the Thatchers, the Sullivans, the Grants – and many others – and Denver had become a very select corner in the world, flaring far and wide, but its light had gone out suddenly.

I had put $1,000 or so in the Peoples National Bank and that was closed, so we were in a poor fix with winter coming on. My horse was still in pasture. I went and brought it home and drove to Fort Collins where I was still well known. The Sherwood Ranch had been sold to a party from Laramie City. They were coming and would build a nice house on the ranch. The old log house on the place was not fit to live in. I waited two weeks for them there. In the meantime, I went hunting north of Collins and had some success. I got several wild geese, ducks and rabbits and shipped them to my folks in Denver. When the owners came, I bargained with them for the house and started to build at once. It was December then. I worked there all winter. I had a few men with me, and we batched in the old log house for it was too far away to come into town every night, about 5 miles. We would not think so now with the automobile, but the automobile was not known then. The 1st of May the work was finished. I got my money. I went back to Denver again - and Denver was still very dull.

Chapter 12

Another Mining Excitement

Cripple Creek was booming. Great gold strikes there, millions taken out of the mines every week. But I was prejudiced against these excitements from my experience in Creed. An architect I knew in Denver had plans to go up there. I bid on the job and got the contract. We went up there – myself and three other men. This was the 1st of November, and we must have some reasonably comfortable quarters to stay in the winter as it is usually pretty sharp in the mountains at that altitude. We built a place large enough for a workshop, a stall for the horse and wagon, and our batching quarters. We were comfortable and everything went well. The winter was mild. We laid bricks every day up to Christmas. The building in question had four stories and there was a lot to it, but we had it completed by the 1st of May.

During the time we were busy with this contract, Cripple Creek was having a boom. The mines were turning out great – a million dollars' worth of ore were shipped out every week and new strikes were made nearly every day. At Anaconda Gulch, a doctor discovered a lead. He located his claim, got some men to work and they loaded a car and shipped it to the smelters. That carload netted $80,000. They called this place the Doctor's Mine. Many mines working then; the Rebecca Mine and the Gold King were located in Poverty Gulch. The Deerhorn and Summit mines were on iron-clad hills, the Elkton mine on Raven Hill. The Bobtail, Anna Lee, Black Diamond, Portland and the Independence were on Battle Mountain. On Bull Hill the Isabella was a heavy producer with many others - the Specimen, the Moose, the Eagles, Orpha May and the Last Dollar. Also, the Teresa and Vindicator. The Anchovia Lelands and Geneva's were on Gold Hill. Also, the Lone Star and the New Moon and a hundred others all shipping in greater or less quantity.

Independence was the most popular mine in the district. W.S. Stratton had located it on the 4th of July and called Independence. Stratton was a poor man when he made the discovery, but as soon as it was seen, he was shipping good ore, buyers came. He sold the mine for half a million dollars, after having paid $80,000. These buyers worked the mine and got enough out to pay them back for the advanced money paid. They lost the lead and gave the mine back to Stratton. He had money now and went to work, relocated the lead, and shipped millions of dollars' worth of goal before selling it again, which he did to an English syndicate for $10 million, it was reported.

In the Cripple Creek district, which included about 10 miles in area, there were several camps or small towns established, Cripple Creek proper, Anaconda, Victor, Gold Hill, Grassys, Altman and Gillette - all wild mining camps.

In Cripple Creek there was a street called Myers Avenue, where every place was either showroom, a show house or a saloon, and Bennett Avenue was a street of stores, hotels, rooming houses and gambling places. Gamblers came from everywhere to get money from Cripple Creek. It really is surprising what an attraction a gambling den has. Like Monte

Carlo which attracts people from all over the world, so did Cripple Creek. They came from England, France, Italy and of course Americans too. In one instance, a young fellow from Philadelphia playing the roulette wheel had won much, but at poker or Faro had lost $15,000, which he could not pay. He promised to send it when he got home. He was slow in doing this. Jim Nolan, who was running The Palace gambling rooms, told Fisher - who had in a way guaranteed the money that if it was not paid - that if the house had lost the money, it would have been paid. Fisher wrote and the Philadelphia man sent the money. Then Fisher said to Nolan, the amount was so large - that he had lost nothing really, and that his friend was willing to pay half of it. Nolan accepted this compromise. It leaked out that all the money had been received, but Fisher had left before they had a chance to get him.

The town was full of mining sharks, selling worthless mines and working all kinds of games. I was afraid of them all, and after finishing my work, I went back to Denver.

But poor Denver had received such a knock-out in the panic of 1893 that it was not fully recovered. There was very little work going on, and new people coming in found enough vacant places to accommodate them. I rested with my family for a while and then later returned to Cripple Creek and opened an office there as an architect. My first job was the electric light plant. That was successful. And I was kept busy planning little houses, stores, hotels etc. Then came the schoolhouses and in a competition for the work I was the successful bidder. I made the plans for five of them, three in Cripple Creek, one in Anaconda and one in Gillette.

A very unfair case was told of a grocer in business in Fall River, MA who had been asked by a young fellow of the same place (who had been in Colorado and had samples of rich ore with him) to grub-stake him. "Give me the money and I will go out and locate a mine and we will share alike in what I find," he said. The grocer furnished the money. The young fellow went back to Cripple Creek and went to work. He soon ran out of money and wrote for more and got it. He kept doing this for more than a year. Then the grocer heard no more from him for some time. He became suspicious and came out to Colorado and to Cripple Creek. He discovered that his partner, the man he had grub-staked, had really struck it pretty rich. He had sold out and was going away. This young fellow was a smart crook, had a lawyer to advise him how to completely beat the grocer. He had everything arranged and had bought his ticket to New York and passage to Europe and was to leave the next day. In the afternoon he and his lawyer went for a little automobile ride to Boulder. Returning, their machine skidded at a turn in the road. The car rolled over and they were both killed. In the young fellow's room at the hotel, his trunk was found to contain $600,000 in currency.

At this time, Cripple Creek was doing fine. Business was good. It was about the best town in Colorado. People flocked in, there were no vacancies. Hotels were over-run and new buildings going up everywhere. It was estimated that 25,000 were crowded into this little town. I had five or six buildings under construction. One was the New Palace Hotel – a good building. It was completed the day before the fire occurred and a grand opening was to be the following day.

Chapter 13

The Cripple Creek Fire

The Portland Hotel was across the street from my office, and looking out the window this day, I saw flames coming out the roof. I ran to see if there I could do anything. People were running out of the hotel shouting "fire," and others were running down from Bennett Ave all shouting "fire, fire!" The Portland was a very cheaply constructed building. The interior was all boarded partitions for the divisions of the rooms and corridors, and this burned in no time at all. Those running from Bennett Avenue had not the time to get down to the fire, one block away, when the roof fell in. The blaze rose more than 100 feet high. The wind was strong and fanned the blaze across Myers Ave. In an instant, that side of the street was on fire and raging through that block as rapidly as a man could walk along the street. People were running in all directions, trying to save something, some carrying clothing, other pieces of furniture and those who had too big a load were overtaken by the sweeping blazes and had to drop it and run to save their lives.

At the corner of Bennett Ave and 2nd St was the Old Palace Hotel. Some suggested "Blow it up!" thinking it would stop the fire. They put several sticks of dynamite under it and exploded it. The entire building went up in the air and then fell to the ground again and there was not a part of it that stood more than four feet above the earth. A minute before it had been a two-story building with 50 rooms on the second floor. This however did not stop the fire. It next attacked the New Palace Hotel and, in a few minutes, it was all ablaze and in a little while nothing was left but the walls, which were of brick and stone. The fire swept from one street to another. There was no chance to fight it for no one could approach anywhere near it. It kept going until the entire west side from 2nd Street burned to the ground. It was a fearful sight. People were crying, they'd lost everything and had no place to go to. The people from the east side came in to help and took those poor wanderers in for the night.

The next morning great crowds started working over all the ruins, not at all discouraged. The weather was good. It was the month of April, but the weather was like June or July.

The Second Fire

A few days later at about 12:00 o'clock there was another shouting, of "fire, fire!" This time, the Show Houses on Myers Ave were afire. It had been stated that the Portland Hotel had been set on fire. That was doubted, but this time around it was fully believed that somebody had purposely started the fire. These buildings on Meyers Avenue were wooden fire traps and burned like straw. The fire swept to Bennett Avenue. By that time, it was so hot that good brick buildings went like wooden ones. I had planned and built a store for the Thompson Dry Goods Co. It was new - just finished. I ran up there and into the building. I said "Let us fight the fire at the windows. The walls will stand alright." But the fire was so hot it burned through the windows and set fire inside. I lingered there, throwing water out the windows trying to keep the fire out. When I saw this was impossible, I ran out at the front of the building. The fire was attacking the rear or from across the alley. When I got to the front the fire was on each side and blowing partly across the street. That part of the town was on the side of the hill, which was too steep to afford a level street. So, a wall was built across the middle and the north side of the street was thus 12 feet higher than the south side. The blazes were leaping over this wall, and I crouched down as low as close into the angle as possible and ran as fast as I could. My clothes and hair were singed before I got through. But for that wall I would have perished trying to save the building.

From there I walked on up on Fourth Street. I had built four nice houses there and I was anxious to save them. There, with the help of others and some water, we kept them from getting afire, although they were pretty well scorched. By this time, nearly the entire town was gone, only bedraggled edges left. Thirty-six square blocks been razed by these two fires, and the inhabitants stood about crowds, hardly saying a world. It was like being at a funeral, thinking of the departed.

Chapter 14

The New Town

I too had a little to think about. The 20 buildings I had planned and built were there in ashes and poor Cripple Creek was surely crippled now. It seemed it would never revive. However, things are not always as they seem, and cripples sometimes come back with renewed life. People began to stir around and said the old fire traps were gone now and good buildings would take their places. Encouragement came from the outside too and money was offered for rebuilding. Business had been good before and it should be better when newly rebuilt and of course be safer.

Stores and rooming houses started building at once. Architects came in from all parts of the country. Inside of two weeks, 20 architects had office is on the grounds and were urging people to build at once while things were cheap. The result was that all were building at once. This made a short boom for the town. People borrowed and built and filled large stores with goods of all kinds. Goods that never sold.

Before the fire, there was a large transient business. That never came back, and the population of the town dwindled down to less than half its former number. The buildings completed, architects and contractors all left. The new stores had very little business. Conditions kept on getting worse. Obligations came due and could not be met. Discouragement set in, people commenced to move out, and matters grew continuously worse.

I had remained and fought for my share of the new buildings and helped my friends as much as I could. When the boom was over, I was the only architect left in the place and that was too many, for there were no more use for even one. The man who was working with me suggested that we get up a picture of the camp with all these new buildings, new streets in the hills surrounding showing the principal mines, etc. The idea was we could sell the pictures and make some money with them. They would advertise the mines and the camp and all that. This fellow was a good painter. He had graduated from school in Germany and knew how to do that kind of work. So, we did get up a large picture (2 ft. high and 3 ft. feet wide) and had it lithographed in several colors. It was a fine piece of work and cost $15,000 for 3000 copies. The lithograph company delayed us for about six months, before delivery. By that time, Cripple Creek had gone broke, and stores were closing their doors. The picture did not sell and turned out to be a total loss.

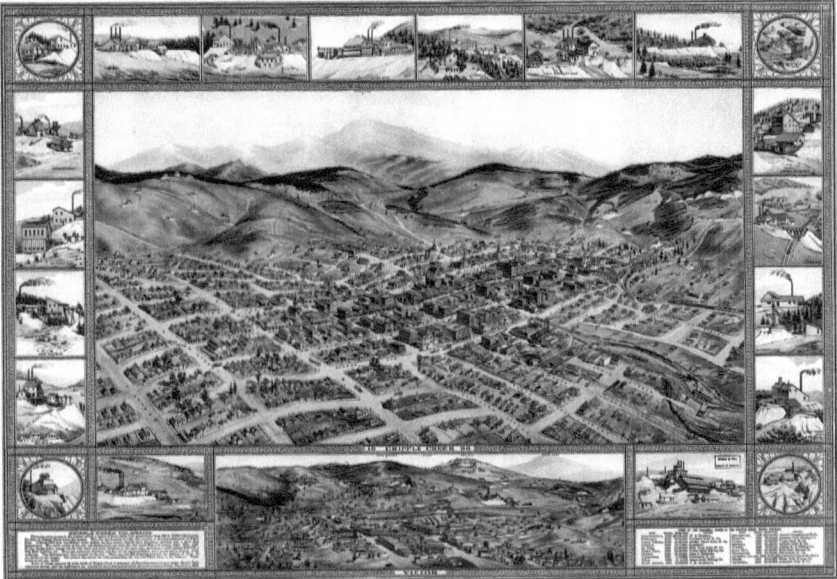

The cover illustration and the image above are reproductions from the US Library of Congress copy of Bernard Dejardin's lithograph of Cripple Creek. You can purchase copies online, so it hasn't been a total loss for some!

Chapter 15

The Rocky Mountains

The Rocky Mountains, my dear reader, means the State of Colorado because the greater part of these rugged ranges is in Colorado. Of the seventy-four peaks of an altitude of over 14,000 feet in the United States, forty-one of them are in Colorado and the scenery they afford is on a greater, more peaceful and lovable scale than in any other part of America. Summers here are sweeter, lovelier, healthier than any other place on this earth, I believe.

The parks, North Park, Middle Park and South Park were the Indians' paradise. They spent their summers there. Game abounded and they had everything to live upon the finest water and air so pure. All these parks are surrounded by high ranges with tops covered nearly all year with perpetual snow. The base of these great peaks and ranges are covered with beautiful forests of pine and quaking aspens, beautiful in their coloring, turning from a light green in summer to yellow and red in the fall. The winters in the mountains are cold, very cold, where the altitude is high on the ranges. Men have perished, attempting to brave the threatening storms at sweeper with the mountains in the winter months.

As previously stated, I was in business in Cripple Creek for two or three years, and as my family was living in Denver, I made trips from Denver to Cripple Creek and returned about every month or so. At Christmas time 1897, I was in Denver. The weather was fine; there had been no snow that fall. I left Denver driving a single horse and a light carriage about 12:00 o'clock noon, having calculated to stop two nights in the road; the first run to take me to Sedalia, the second night to Woodland Park, and the next stop Cripple Creek. The entire trip is about 125 miles. That was a pretty long drive for one horse, but I drove slow, and stopped a number of times so that the horse stood it as well as I.

I had intended to return right away from Cripple Creek, but the business I had on hand was delayed and I had to stay there for over a week. The weather being fine on the 29th of December, Mr. Aubrey, a friend, and I walked up to Mount Pisgah, a distance of about four miles. We climbed to the top of the peak to see the country beyond. The view from there was really fine. At a distance of a few miles lies the valley of Four Mile Creek and below the rolling hills to Cañon City, about 25 miles away. Then the Black Mountains west of Cañon City, 40 miles away from Cripple Creek. Further West and South, the great Sangre de Christo range is about 100 miles away from Cripple Creek, yet in plain view, as if not half that far. This is a wonderful great range its top white with snow and the blue forests at the base. About the center of this range is one of the highest peaks in the state called Sierra Blanca. At the left, not very far from this range are two Spanish peaks. They are beautifully formed in cone-like shape, with tops finished with white tips, not unlike the pyramids of Egypt, only much larger of course. This was the view that we had from the top of the Pisgah. It was grand and beautiful.

On the 31st of December I succeeded in settling my affairs and made ready to leave early in the morning for Denver. I fed my horse late in the night so I could leave as soon as I got up. I arose at 5:00 o'clock and harnessed the horse and left.

Just as I started, it began snowing. I did not like that very well, but I thought if I could not get through, I would stop somewhere and went on. I drove up Tenderfoot Hill and on the way to Gillette daylight came and the snow fell heavier than before.

We passed Gillette and went down to Midland about 16 miles from Cripple Creek. There I stopped and fed the horse and took some breakfast myself. I felt I needed food to keep me warm; then I hitched up again and left. It was still snowing. I then drove on to Hayden divide, eight miles further. There I stopped again. I did not like the camp, so after resting a few minutes I drove on to Woodland Park - another eight miles.

Here I unharnessed and fed the horse and took some lunch. We stayed there for two hours. The snow was now about four inches or more on the ground. I was undecided then as the way I should go, either by way of the Ute Pass or over the range to Palmer Lake. I thought that this trail might be bad with the snow, which it was, but it was 25 miles shorter to Denver by Palmer Lake then going by way of Ute Pass. I had gone up the trail and knew it well so decided to go over the range. I figured that I could get across by 10 or 11 o'clock, rest at Palmer Lake for the balance of the night, and go on to Denver the next day.

The distance from Woodland Park to Palmer Park Lake is 18 miles on this trail, which runs over the Front Range at an altitude of around 10,000 feet. At 3:30 or so, we left Woodland Park and traveled to the foot of the range at the edge of Manitou Park.

Before beginning to climb on the range, I noticed that my horse showed signs of fatigue. I unhitched him again, rubbed him good, fed him oats, chopped the ice on a little stream at my right and got water to give him a drink. I then allowed him to rest for about an hour. It was about 7:00 o'clock by then. We had only gone about five miles from Woodland Park. It had stopped snowing, but it was turning cold. The wind was blowing, and the snow was drifting some.

I could not stay there for the night and did not wish to go back to Woodland Park, so I hitched the horse again and we started to climb the range. The snow was about six inches deep then on the level ground. This did not bother very much and as long as the road went through timber, we had no trouble.

I had dressed myself warm, wearing woolen underwear, woolen socks, a heavy woolen sweater over my shirt, coat and overcoat. I wore high shoes and had taken the precaution to wrap my feet with several layers of newspaper and draw over that the storm rubbers. This proved to be very wise, and I did not suffer with cold feet, cold as it got later on.

When we passed the timber and reached what we call "near timberline," we found the snow had drifted in the low places. The short gullies - 20 to 50 yards or so - had drifts one to two feet high and the horse could not lift his legs over. I had to get down and track the snow in front of him in a little channel so he could pass. In that way we went on and the further we went, the more often this deep snow occurred. Finally it got to be covered with snow, I could not see the road well, and the wheel of the carriage ran over a rock and the thing tipped over. The shaft pressing against the horse's leg annoyed him and he kicked until he broke the shaft. But I thought if he could kick so well, he was good yet and hitched him up again and we went on somewhat farther.

By that time, it was about 12:00 o'clock midnight. It was very cold. The snow in the gullies was hard and the horse was so tired that he lay down in the snow and refused to get up. I unhitched him and gave him some oats, but he would not eat, so I let him rest. As I too was getting tired, I sat in the snow to rest, thinking of the next best thing to do, when I fell asleep.

I did not sleep long, however; I was awakened as if someone had touched me. The cold was sizzling and noises like pistol shots rang from every direction. I could not explain at first the cause of these seeming shots, but later on I reasoned it out this way:

Several years before, there had been a growth of timber on this range. The trees are short and scrubby with heavy trunks, because this was near timberline. When the fire passed, these trees were left standing. They had died and in drying they cracked open, the cracks being more than one inch wide sometimes. In time, these trees fell down. The snow had started as wet snow and had filled these crevices with water and when the frost came, the ice in expanding cracked the wood open with a noise like a shot. So it was not ghosts after all.

By this time the horse was also up and eating snow. I hitched him up again and started in the same manner as before, hoping that I would soon arrive at the Balanced Rock. This was a large boulder, 25 or 30 feet high, which had but a very small base and - leaning to one side - seemed it might roll over at any moment. It stands at the top of the long hill above Palmer Lake and about 6 miles from that place. I thought if I reached the rock, the rest of the way would be downhill and the horse would have no trouble pulling us down. But we did not get to it.

The horse was exhausted and would go no farther. I decided to abandon the carriage and try to make the horse save me. I knew that if I did not get to Palmer Lake, I would freeze to death, and no one would know where to look for me. No one knew the way I'd gone. I stripped the harness from the horse, gave him a good rubbing on the body and the legs and left only the bridle on him. I took the lap robe and put it on his back and talked to him as if he understood me. Maybe he did.

"Now Bill," I said, "if you save me, I will save you. So, pluck up old boy and we will be alright." I tried to get on his back, but I could not make it.

In tramping down the snow to make channels for the horse the snow had gotten under my trousers up to the knees and had melted, of course, with the heat in my body. Now it was frozen so stiff I could not spring enough to get on the horse. I led him for a while until I found a rock and by stepping on it, I mounted the him, and we went on.

It was now 1:30 AM and bitterly cold. Frost was in the air, and I could not see well; although the moon was out, I could only get half a vision of things, which made it very difficult to follow the road. It all looked so wild and dreary. I was getting to the point of complete exhaustion when we arrived at the Balanced Rock. I saw it with a joy I cannot describe. It had something to do with our chances of getting to Palmer Lake.

"Hello old boulder," I said, "I see you're still waiting for us. How do you like the weather?" I got no answer, but it had a friendly appearance anyway. At this point we were still over 10,000 feet high but starting down the hill to Palmer Lake. This hill is 4 miles long and winds around in such a way to give a reasonable grade.

At places the road is cut in to the side of the hill in a triangular shape. When we got to such places, the horse walked near the edge where the snow was not deep. It was then that I realized my good fortune that I did not come down with the buggy. If I had, the horse walking near the edge would have put the wheel over, and we would have rolled down to the bottom several hundred feet below.

When we got to the foot of the hill, we came to the Tie Camp. I had seen this camp when I went up. There were many men there then so I thought that I might stop there and lodge with them. I got off the horse and walked over to the cabin. It was deserted. The door was open in and the snow had drifted in so that it laid on the floor as high as the bunks.

The party had gone home for the holidays. I returned to the horse. He was waiting for me. I managed to get on him again and we went on to Palmer Lake, some two miles further.

A few years before I had built an addition to the Rockland Hotel at Palmer Lake. While there, I boarded at Mr. Younger's house. I knew him well, so I went there now and asked to be let in. When he asked who was there, I told him. He came down and opened the door and I said, "Good morning, Mr. Younger." He asked where I came from, I told him, and he could hardly believe it. "I thought you had good sense," he remarked.

It was four o'clock then, and when he reached out to see his thermometer, it showed 24 degrees below zero. It must have been very much lower than that on the mountain. Mr. Younger built a good fire in the stove, and while I thawed the ice from my ankles and knees by putting him over the stove, he went out and put my horse in the stable. He came back and got me something to eat. He thought I must be frozen, but I was not. I then went to bed and slept until 10:00 o'clock. When I got up, I went out and found a man with a horse to go after my carriage, which I had left in the mountains.

I took a saddle horse for myself and went along. The weather was clear, and the mountains looked beautiful with the white snow from the day before. We found the wreck and it looked like a shipwreck, with only part of it to be seen. It was about one and a half miles beyond the Balanced Rock. The drifts had covered the carriage completely, only the back of the seat, top of the wheels and the whip were sticking out of the snow.

We shoveled the snow, hitched his big horse on, and started to return. Going down, we tipped over twice, but managed to get down the hill and to Palmer Lake. There I harnessed up my horse and left for Denver. I traveled 10 miles that evening and stopped at Mr. Cantrill's place for the night.

The following morning, I left early and reached Denver by night. Everyone was well at home. The children, seeing me, said "Papa where have you been? You were not home for Christmas, and we had such a fine time - the best Christmas we ever had." So, they were happy and I was pleased. I did not tell them how near they had come to not seeing me again. I soon forgot about it myself.

Chapter 16

Life in Colorado

Boulder was stirring itself and trying to get up a building excitement. Real estate men were planning new additions and advertising the town. I went there, rushed around, and found that those that were building. I made plans for an addition to and remodeling of the Boulder National Bank, and this brought me other work. I built eight buildings there in that summer. Before completing them in the fall. I was taken sick and came home to my family in Denver. I had a bad case of typhoid fever. It went hard with me. I had a double run of fever and was not able to get up for nine weeks. When I had recovered sufficiently, I went to Boulder and settled all matters there, then returned to Denver.

Work was opening up in Denver as well here, and I soon got very busy with contracts, leaving out the architecture for contracting was more profitable. This was during the period of war with Spain - when the papers said war was declared between Spain and the United States. It probably would be a good scrap, the English papers said, and it would not be all one sided either. I don't know what England said after Spain had lost Cuba and the Philippines - and the United States not losing a man in the fight.

Times were good then. Times are always good during periods of war. War is a revival in case of hard times – but the aftermath often leaves matters worse than they were before.

In the years following, I found myself engaged in much work. Denver was full of work - for everybody. I was busy on my work - and at home too - for we had twins come to us and I can say that twins make one pretty busy.

Business went on fine for a while - until the workers asked for more pay and shorter hours. They went on strike and tied up all the construction work in the city. This strike lasted for four months and caused great loss to all parties concerned.

Labor, of course, is fundamental for all production. It is more fundamental than capital, but it must be so regulated that capital will be attracted for reasonable gain on its investment. Labor sometimes goes too far and harms itself as well as others. The American Federation of Labor was organized in 1880. Then came the Amalgamated Labor union or Trades Union. The purpose was to raise wages and keep Chinese labor out of the country. The Knights of Labor was formed as a society with insurance benefits. In time, the labor unions found more favor with the working men and grew very fast, while the Knights of Labor went down to near nothing. In 1905, the federation had two million members and became a power. They dictated the policy of the government as far as they could through their representatives and forced their views on an unwilling public. Organized boycotts were put into effect and all classes of laborers taken into the ranks. Assessments were levied and used for sympathetic strikers. Strikers in Colorado were receiving money from the Union in other parts of the country so they could hold out and win the strike, and vice versa for other occasions. The results were pretty sure to be in favor of the Unions.

I had a contract on a business block, a four-story building. As the strike was called, the men left the work. I could not afford the increase in wages that was asked and attempted to carry on with non-union men. That was a bad job. The men I could get were not skilled. I worked with them, but it was not possible to keep things going right. One day a man let a load fall from a derrick. A part of it fell on me and broke my left arm between the wrist and the elbow. The blow knocked me down, but I got up and walked off to a doctor. He put splints in my arm and fixed me a sling to hold it up and two hours later, I was back at work again.

I managed to keep the work going for a while by being on the job every day and was really too busy to think about my arm. I got along fairly well, but at night I suffered much. This strike was general. All other constructions in the city were in about the same fix as I. One day I made up my mind that I had held off long enough. I went before the committee, and told them so. I said, we are keeping up a losing fight and we better compromise. This was effected, and the strike was called off.

My arm soon healed up. I continued working and built three other blocks that fall. And activity followed the same business for several years, always in sharp competition. Sometimes making money, sometimes losing money - for contracting is a gamble, and it fluctuates more or less depending on the markets as well as upon labor.

Chapter 17

Vacation out East

In the summer of 1906, we went for a visit to my old home, this time, not alone. My wife and the twins made a party of four, including myself. We traveled by train to Buffalo, NY and then by boat on Lake Erie and down the Saint Lawrence to Quebec, then to Andreville (or St. Andre was the name when I was a boy). My father was 80 years old then, but in good health. We stayed there a few weeks, then returned to Denver by the same route. We had a nice vacation and saw some interesting sights. While at Buffalo we visited Niagara Falls and walked under waters falling from a height of 150 feet; the waters falling away from the rocky wall and leaving a space underneath large and dry enough to walk under for some distance. Guides led us and charged $0.50 a person and of course many have visited there.

Resuming the work where I had left it, I soon got several contracts on my hands and the labor agitation started again. The businessmen of the city favored labor, thinking that contractors made lots of money and ought to pay labor well. Labor was well paid, but they demanded more, and shorter hours. A dollar an hour they must have, and they got it. The people had to pay it. The contractor had to charge higher prices for their work. This is soon felt and the public quit building and another depression swept the country again. I finished the work I had on hand and took another vacation.

Bernard designed and built the Russell family home in Southport, CT. The columns were salvaged from a decommissioned church. As of this writing, the house still stands.
Russell Family Archives

From Washington, we traveled by boat to New York, down the Potomac to Norfolk, VA. We saw Fortress Monroe and Hampton Beach, where the Merrimack and Monitor fought. The Monitor was not there. It was out of style, and Uncle Sam has new ones now, more stylish ones and up to date.

We went in to swim at Virginia Beach Park. We tried to go into a park and were refused entrance at the gates. When I asked the reason, the negro attendant said, "This here park is a colored park."

From Norfolk to New York on the Old Dominion Steamer, a lovely trip and the entrance into New York was fine. We stayed in New York a few days and went to Coney Island. I went in the surf with the crowds, but my wife would not go. She was afraid of the sea.

From New York, we went up the Hudson to Plattsburgh and across Lake Champlain to Burlington, VT and visited relatives there. Then onto the old home in Canada to see my father again. Father was sick then. He had had a stroke from which he died a while later. This was the last time I saw him.

When Bernard Desjardins retired in the 1930's, he traveled in France and bought several clocks for which he made elaborate cases.

Hume Family Archives

Chapter 18

The Deer Hunt

On September 29, 1907, I left Denver with a companion I will call Jos. We were bound for North Park and Routt County on a deer hunt. We went by train to Fort Collins, taking the stage to Log Cabin where we stayed for the night.

The stage was a poor conveyance, very slow, and it was cold, and it snowed all the way. In order to keep warm, I had to jump out and walk. When going uphill it was easy to keep up with the horses. We were nine hours going 40 miles. In that time, we stopped at Livermore where we had lunch.

Log Cabin was not a comfortable place. The lady proprietor seemed to have so many things to attend to that she could not find time to make us comfortable and we tramped around in the snow and cold wind for more than an hour before she decided that we could come in. Then she had so much to say that I can only recall that she was very anxious to get away from there and that she was very large.

The next morning, not being able to get transportation, we walked to Smith's place five miles on. There was snow and mud on the road which made bad walking. At Smith they would not take us in or feed us, and we went on five miles farther to Wilson's Place.

This place was called West Lake. We stayed there all night. I had just gotten a new pair of hunting boots and they made my heels so sore that I could hardly keep them on my feet. The following morning, we tried to get someone to take us over the range onto the Laramie River, but could not, so we left at about 7 o'clock and walked to the top of the divide where we ran across some campers and had lunch with them. We continued on our way to the Laramie River and stopped at the Glen-Davey Ranch. We stayed there two days on account of my feet. Jos went out to look for deer, but saw none.

The following day I got a saddlehorse and rode over the range near the head of the Laramie River, but saw no deer.

The next day again we left at seven a.m. and walked to the McIntyre River, about four miles, stopping at Tallmadge's cabin. Mr. Tallmadge was not in, but a fellow stopping there said he was sure Tallmadge would be glad to take us in for a few days. We rested for a while, then went out to look for deer on the slopes of the Medicine Bow Range, but saw none. We both returned to the cabin about the same time, very hungry. We asked the young fellow if he could give us something to eat. He did and Tallmadge came in about 7 o'clock. When he saw we had eaten before he came, he seemed to be very angry, and we could not get a word out of him the entire evening.

I tried a dozen times to sort of tame him by saying nice things about his cabin, that it was well planned and had pretty surroundings etc., but it was not until late that we could get his dander down so he would talk. He finally promised to drive us over the range in the morning.

There was no room on the first floor, so we slept in the attic; no stairs, but they put up a ladder and we climbed up. There was no bed, only blankets on the floor on which to sleep. I did not sleep well and at about 5:00 o'clock we heard Mr. Tallmadge downstairs. We got up and went down and he seemed to be grouchy again. He told us he would not take us over the range.

He gave no reason - had just changed his mind.

I did not think well of that and sent Jos back to Glen Davey to have them send a team. My foot was still sore, and I could not undertake walking 20 miles in that condition. When the team arrived from Glen Davey and Mr Tallmadge saw us leave, he was very angry.

The team took us to the top of the range and would go no farther. We had to walk the balance of the way about 12 miles to a ranch. The Two-Bar ranch. This was a cattle ranch, and the cattle were branded with two bars on the left side, hence the name. From this place we could see much of the park (North Park). Very pretty to look at but not so good to walk over. It was a hard tramp in loose sand, and we made it only two miles an hour.

We arrived at the ranch at three o'clock. The men there refused us food on account of the absence of the bosses. We did not know what to do but rest and wait until the bosses arrived. About an hour later a team drove in with two ladies. One was the wife of the boss and the other her friend.

We had to be gallant and by as much flattery as I could think of, we got something to eat and spent the evening very nicely, playing cards and telling stories. We had a good bed sleep in. We left the Two-Bar ranch early the following morning and walked in to Walden, the capital city of North Park.

This town had about 300 inhabitants. We found some people I knew and were taken care of while there. We had our room at Mr. Rodgers' house. This man had worked for me some years before. He was a good man, but subject to epilepsy. He had been in a very bad condition; often he took these fits daily, so that he could not hold his job. He had a wife and children, and they were very poor. They went about the country in a wagon with an old nag of a horse, very much like gypsies.

In the summer they had traveled into the Park and camped on the creek just outside the town. Mrs. Rodgers went in to town to do washing. Her work was so well done that the people took an interest in the family and made them come to town, helped them get a house, and from then on prosperity stayed with the Rodgers family. Mr. Rogers told me he had never had an epileptic fit since coming to the Park. He believed it was on account of the altitude and said that he was doing quite well. The children were growing and helping. He had teams and was doing freighting from Laramie City to the Park and Mrs. Rogers ran a hotel. I was glad to see them happy and prosperous

There lived in North Park at that time, a fellow they called "Rattlesnake Pete." He made a business of killing coyotes. This is the manner which he did his work; when he saw a wolf go into a hole in the ground, he would shove his boy - a very small lad - in after him to tie a rope around the leg of the coyote and Rattlesnake Pete would then pull the boy out with the rope tied to his leg thus pulling the coyote out and would kill it.

We stayed in Walden for two days. North Park is a fine place to visit in the summer. The altitude of the park is about 8,000 feet. It has very small several small rivers with clear water, well stocked with trout. This water is from the snowy peaks that completely surround the Park.

Looking around, one would think that at one time it must have been a good-sized lake. It's about 45 miles wide with about 65 miles long. The ranges have snow all summer long and they look beautiful, particularly Medicine Bow range. This name was given by the Indians who went there to get the mountain ash for their bow. To the Indians, "Medicine" meant good or the best.

Leaving Walden, we got a ride to Hebron and stayed there all night at Mr. McConnaughy's. He had a fine ranch. The house stood at the junction of two nice streams called the Large and Small Grizzlies. We were well received. These people as a rule like to have visitors from Denver. As a result, we were treated well, and our expenses were very reasonable.

We left there early in the morning on our way to Bennett's sawmill at the foot of the Continental Divide. Finding a place where we could stop, we climbed the range. We were on a high ridge, and we could see the Park we had left in the morning and a fog hung over it. With the bright sunshine above it, it looked like a lake with ranges all around it.

At 1:30 we were on the main range over what was called Buffalo Pass. The roads there in the timber were very bad. There had been much snow the previous week and this was melting and running, so we commenced to get a little worried about the distance we had to cover to reach Steamboat Springs as there was no place we could stay between Hebron and Steamboat Springs.

When we reached the top of the Pass, I felt pretty tired. I had on heavy clothing, carried many things, a gun, a scout axe, a Kodak camera, a satchel, and other things of necessity. The weight of this outfit was about 30 pounds. This becomes very heavy when one is tired.

A little ways farther on, we were met by a team coming from Steamboat Springs. They told us it was twelve miles to the Springs, but there was a cut-off that we could take. If we went on for a mile farther, we could see a town between two hills. At that place, we could leave the road and take one that would lead us directly to Steamboat Springs and save us about 5 miles. We went on, and as they said, we saw the town and left the main road starting to cut across.

If this had been earlier in the day, it would have been alright, but it was near sunset and soon after we started down, darkness came upon us. We followed a small creek, Fish Creek I believe it's called, until it led us into a narrow cañon with sides so steep we could not walk on them.

Walking up the edges of the creek at one place, we could not have gone through had it not been for the fallen trees that had rolled down and enmeshed themselves into a sort of covering over the creek. This was very slow travel, the hours passed, and we were getting hungry. Finally, the banks of the creek seemed to be not quite steep, and we walked a short distance, expecting to get better walking. Yet it was so steep, we had to hang on to the bushes. These bushes were prickly and made our hands sore. They picked us through our clothing on the arms and legs.

It was getting pretty tough. Just then, Jos was leading a few paces ahead - we could not see each other it was so dark. Suddenly he said he called and said "Quick! Take my gun." I advanced a little and took his gun. He said, "Don't come any farther. There's a hell of a hole here." He was hanging onto a bush or root. I put our guns down, gave him my hand, and helped him up - and for curiosity lighted a match to see what the hole was. It was a slide in the side of the hill, 50 feet wide or more and probably 100 feet to the Creek below.

Jos was frightened. He said, "I can go no further," and his voice was trembling. It was then about 8 o'clock. A little later, the moon rose, and soon after that we could see our way. I said to Jos, "sit down awhile," and we rested for a few minutes. Then I suggested we go up above the slide and go cautiously to a more level place where we could rest. We did this, and as we went up, we noticed that it sloped down gradually as we went on.

A few moments later, we heard the sound of water again and soon got to the Creek. A little ways from there we found the headgate of a small ditch. I said, "Now we're alright. All we have to do is follow the ditch. This will bring us to some man's home."

We followed this for a mile or more. The moon was up then and we could see fairly well. A moment later we saw the lights of Steamboat Springs. At a distance, it appeared to us to be not more than two miles. Jos suggested that we cut across. Of course, we were pretty well above the town. I thought that we should stay with ditch, but Jos' judgment was that we cut across. He wasn't fully over his scare and was anxious to get somewhere.

It was a steep hill with much fallen timber and those prickly bushes again and we soon lost sight of the town. That proved to me that there was still another mountain between us and the town. We could not go back to find our ditch, so we went on and after dragging ourselves for an hour or more, we got around this mountain and again saw the lights about a mile away. We were free then, but exhausted. I think it took us an hour to walk the last mile. We got into Steamboat Springs about 11:00 PM. Noticing a light on a veranda, which we thought was a hotel sign, we investigated and found it to be the Onyx Hotel. We went in and asked for a room and something to eat.

There were plenty of rooms but no eats. The cook was gone; and no one there knew anything about cooking. I asked for the proprietor and a man answered, saying he was one we were looking for. I told him if he would show me the door to the kitchen, I was sure I could find something. I also told him we were from Denver and had to have at least one meal a day or were liable to collapse.

I told the story of our experiences. Our twenty-eight mile walk over the range and many miles around the mountains in the dark. The man gave in and led us to the kitchen. We found a pot on the kitchen range with a good portion of a chicken stew which had been left from the evening meal, some coffee, bread, jam, and apples. Gee! But it was a fine meal. "You can't beat it." I said, "I don't care what you got." Our host said he could not get eggs. He blamed the farmers saying the chickens would lay alright, but they did not care for them properly. "Why," he said, "I bought some chickens the other day and I got 19 eggs, but of course I fixed them right. I made nice boxes for them to lay in, yes I did, and by George nine of them went and laid in the grass." Jos remarked "Is that so? Well that just shows what kind of raising they had!" Jos had lost part of his wits in the mountain, but was recovering them now. He was over his scare, had a good meal, and was enjoying himself. So was I, and I believe our host did too.

We were so tired the next day all we did was to visit around the town. We saw the springs from which the town received its name. The action of the spring is a gushing from a hole in the ground and as this water and steam comes out it makes a whistling sound like that of a steamboat whistle. We also took baths in the hot springs, the waters being very warm and spent the remainder of the day resting and went to bed early.

The next morning, we took the stage for Hahn's Peak, the famous gold field which brought so many people out West, seeking riches. They did not all become rich, however. From what I saw, I believe many millions were spent in mining, but few millions were taken out. The district was what is called "placer ground," covering about one mile square. It had all been worked out; in some places, perhaps 50 feet deep, but there was no more work being done at the time.

There was nothing of interest here outside the mining, so we did not stay but returned to Steamboat by the same stage. The next day we staged at Yampa and Rock Creek, staying at Rock Creek overnight.

This is at the base of the Gore range and at the east end of Routt County, the largest county in the state of Colorado and probably the richest.

There's enough coal there, a very fine grade of bituminous, to furnish the whole United States for 500 years, and oil too; farming and cattle, game of all kinds. If you want bears, or lions, wildcats, or deer there are plenty of them all; just go and get them. It's not far from Denver, only 200 miles. The Moffat railroad takes you there in six or eight hours, or you can go by automobile. The roads are fine all the way.

The following morning, we left Rock Creek on foot looking for deer and traveling towards Kremmling over the Gore range. Jos took one way to the east and I went west, leaving a distance between ourselves. So, if I scared any game his way, he would get it and if they came my way, I was to get them. But neither of us got any. Jos did not see any. I saw one deer that Jos must have scared but he passed me by like lightning. Never have I seen anything nicer. I heard him coming and made ready to shoot, but when I saw him, I changed my mind and let him pass. He was the prettiest animal imaginable, bounding in leaps of fifteen or twenty feet. His four, fine, thin legs and little hoofs touched the ground at the same time. His head was high, and he went so fast he seemed as if flying half the time I thought what a pity it is to kill deer and have never been after them since.

After seeing this deer, I did not look for any others. I was converted as far as killing deer was concerned, so I looked for ore specimens. I was on the Gore range that had a reputation for mines and was supposed to contain some rich ore deposits. I found several pieces of float, an indication of ore veins, which made me believe that a good mining proposition would be found there some day.

My intention was to go to Kremmling, but the day was cloudy. I did not see the sun and had lost my direction, going too far West. About 1:00 o'clock I was on top of the range and some distance away. I saw smoke in the timbers. I went to it. This was Wilson's sawmill. I had some lunch there and rested a while. The men told me it was 13 miles to Penny's Ranch where Jos and I were to meet that night, and nine miles to Kremmling. So, I decided to walk to Kremmling. I arrived at the hotel at 7:00 o'clock after walking about 30 miles that day. I was pretty tired, but not any more than when I had walked the first 18 miles. I was getting used to it.

Fearing that Jos would worry about me, I called the Penny Ranch by telephone and found he had arrived there. He said he would come in to Kremmling in the morning. He had 16 miles to walk. It was ten o'clock the next morning when he arrived, and this ended our walking. We took the Moffat train home that afternoon, arriving in Denver in the evening.

We did not kill any dear. I don't know how Jos felt about it, but I was glad of it. We had the experience and that was better for us. I felt the good of the good effect of that trip all through the winter.

I got back to Denver again and Denver was doing very little building. The city was getting much from the mines. All the ores, or nearly all came to the Denver smelters, the Argo Smelters, the Globe smelters, and other smaller ones and many samplers. The ores came from Cripple Creek, Leadville, Silverton, Boulder, and other places. About $100 million worth of the different minerals came into Denver each year. That helped keep the city alive, but it was not enough to cause them to do much building, so most of the builders had very little to do.

Chapter 19

The State of Colorado

Just one hundred years after the declaration of independence, Colorado was received into the Union as a state, and is therefore called the Centennial State. Because I have passed the greater part of my life here, I may be pardoned for wandering from my story, in relating some of its early history, particularly about Denver. The records show that the first invasion of what is now the State of Colorado was by trappers. They were after the fur of beavers, minks, fox, etc. They thought nothing of the farming or the mining, or of staying on the land.

Then came the expeditions sent out by the Government. Lieutenant Pike, Major Long, Doctor James, Kit Carson, and others. They were in the country at an early date, but were only transient, and not pioneers.

The pioneers were those who came seeking gold. The lure of gold brought them here. To get rich and return home was their aim. They did not think of colonizing the country. But the travel over this wide country, its hardships and dangers were too great to attempt to return - few ever did. Though not finding gold as plentiful as expected, they chose to stay. Gold was found by panning the sand and gravel in the streams, but not in great quantity, and the miners and prospectors had to be provided for. So, villages were built up and these became the pioneers' homes.

The cost of importing supplies being so great they set to cultivating the land and farming prospered. The water of the streams used for irrigation proved to be the best asset to the farmer, and the agriculture in Colorado produces more per acre under cultivation than even the good lands of the middle states, or perhaps of any place, and stock-raising soon became the largest asset to the country.

Mining developed rapidly. Gold and silver were found in different parts of the hills, Georgetown, Central City, Leadville, and many other places. Many towns were built over the state, but Denver led in population. It soon was apparent it was destined to be the best and largest city in the state. The lay of the land was just right for a large city. Its climate was the finest known, and the view of the mountains from here a real joy to those who lived here.

The first settlement, which is now a part of Denver, was called Araria, located on the Platte River about five miles south of the present city. Later it developed lower down on the river at the juncture of the Platte with Cherry Creek. Trails across the prairies led up the South Platte to Cherry Creek, and the caravans of covered wagons stopped there. So, the village soon grew into a town. When it was incorporated into a city it was called Denver. In the early history of the place there were many renegades, escaped criminals and low types. When they were found out, justice was swift, and many culprits were found hanging from the limbs of trees and buried near the place.

In the years following 1860 the better men became more conspicuous, and they were needed. In 1864 the Indians made real war on the white people and a reign of terror took place through all the land from the Rocky Mountains to the Missouri

River. Bands of Indians waited for the stages and robbed and killed the travelers. Covered wagon caravans were attacked on all trails. No road was safe. The Government was called upon to give assistance but the war between the North and the South was not yet terminated. Governor Evans and Elbert, and others, desired to drive the Indians out and gave them a trouncing. The result was that peace and security was established.

The real Builders of Denver and the State, Governor John Evans, David H. Moffat and William N. Byers, were most conspicuous and brought honor to the State and to the City.

The climate in Colorado is probably as good as any place in the world. Can you imagine anything nicer and better than the cool breeze of a summer night here, blowing down on the prairies from the snow-covered mountains? And the altitude too, which makes the air so light and clear, where one can see one hundred and fifty to two hundred miles. The beauty of the mountains too. While there are higher mountains in other places, the Rocky Mountains are tame and inviting, where comfort and peace seem to be a part of them. Cañon after cañon with crystal clear water running between gentle sloping hills, with evergreen pines at all seasons.

Colorado is called the playground of America, but it is only fairly started in development. The state, with the aid of the United States Government, is building roads in many of the places where the beauty of the great Ranges can be enjoyed. The roads to the top of Pikes Peak and Mount Evans, now completed, are surely grand. The Fall River Pass and a dozen other passes from ten to twelve thousand feet in altitude, are but a part of the Great Attraction one feels as he gets acquainted with the mountains.

There is some real game in the mountains of Colorado. The deer, the elk and mountain sheep. There are some nearly everywhere in the hills, and it is fine to see them at home. They look so pretty and content - what we would call happy. One almost envies them the blissful life they live. There are the mountain bears too, and the mountain lions, very bad fellows, but they seldom come down below timber line - and people seldom go above that.

The time will surely come when many beautiful resorts will be used by people from all parts of the country.

Chapter 20

A Sea of Mountains

In my first summer here, I had a chance to get acquainted with the mountains and hills of the Rockies. At home I had been a good mountain-climber, but our hills were a few hundred feet high. Here the hills were several thousand feet high, and it required some knowledge of them before one could climb them successfully.

My first real experience in the hill-climbing was on a trip to the Rist Canon above La Porte, about 2,000 ft of a climb. The hill was very steep, and before I reached the top, I was so winded that I was not sure whether I would make it or tumble down to disaster. I made it, however, but I had to lie down for a time after reaching the top, for my heart was beating as if I had been running a great race.

It was from this place that the memory of my dream I had as a boy came to me, for the view of the prairies from this place was what I had seen in my dream. The prairies, seen from that elevation, appeared to lay flat and level as a lake - as far as I could see - vanishing in the distance there was not a tree anywhere except along the river bottoms, where the cottonwoods and the boxelders grew. But the entire country outside of that was barren. One would hardly believe it today for the country where irrigation is applied, the landscape is alive with beautiful clusters of trees that have been planted in such manner as to give protection and beauty as well.

After this experience my desire for climbing increased. I joined a party to climb Pikes Peak. There were four in our party. Mr. Spearling from Chicago, the artist who was painting scenes and decorations in the New Broadway Theater, with two of his men, and myself. We went by train to Manitou which is at the foot of the Peak. Arriving there at 7:30 P.M., we started to walk up on the trail. This was before the Cog Railroad was built. The distance from Manitou to the top of the trail is 12 miles, and very steep. It required from 6 to 8 hours to reach the top. Mr. Spearling had planned it out. We were to walk on up to the half-way house, rest there for a while, then go on to the rest of the way before sunrise. The idea was to see the sunrise from above, showing daylight in the distance, with darkess still on at the foot of the peak. This, of course, makes the curvature of the earth quite visible, which is a really thrilling spectacle.

After walking for four hours, we arrived at the halfway house. We had some coffee there and retired for a short rest. At 2:30 we started again, but the climb became slower and slower as we got higher, and the sun came up to the horizon before we reached the top of the Peak. Mr. Spearling was sorry for that, but it could not be helped. We had stopped too long at the half-way house. We were not experienced mountain-climbers, and our advance was slow. We were three hours making the last 1,000 feet, having to sit down or lie down every few rods to give the heart a rest, for it was beating at such a rate that we all were scared.

We reached the top at about 9 o'clock instead of four as we had planned, but the view that we got from there was good enough to pay for our troubles. There was an inn or hotel up there, where one could stay and get something to eat. After eating and resting awhile we started to go down. There were some small white clouds stirring around the Peak below us. As we went down these turned into rain and poured down on us for three or four miles. We were soaking wet. Then as we got below the clouds, the sun was shining. Reaching Manitou our clothes were dry again. Our train came soon after, and we went on board for Denver. It had been an ideal trip and a very pleasant experience.

Later the Colorado Mountain Club was organized, and I joined the Club. I was now a real enthusiastic mountain-climber, and we had outings every week, taking the principal ranges and peaks in all parts of the state, and, of course, we learned how to go about it. Walking up to 14,000 or 15,000 feet altitude is not so hard if one knows how. It has to be taken slowly and time given for the heart to adjust itself, which it does unless one gets excited and gets mountain-sickness, which is similar to seasickness in some ways. Our experiences were that the trips were beneficial, except in a very few cases, where the persons were not in proper condition for it.

Some of the peaks that are easy to climb and worthwhile are Pikes, Long, Mount Evans, Gray, Tory, James, the Arapahoes, Audubon, Clarence King, McClelland, Thorodin, the North and South Boulder Peaks and others of lesser height. These are all in the Front Range, and visible from Denver, and the trip to any of them can be made in one day. Other ranges - the Park Range, Mosquito Range, the Collegian Ranges, Sawatch Range, Continental Range (called the Divide) all have beautiful snow-crested peaks, that are inviting beyond imagination. To see the Mount of the Holy Cross, Mount Massive, Elbert, Princeton, Harvard, Yale, and Lincoln, is of greatest delight to anyone.

These are but a few of the marvelous peaks one can see here, for there are more than 200 of them, 40 of them exceeding 14,000 ft. in height - and hundreds of hills, 1,000 to 3,000 or 4,000 feet high, beautifully shaded with aspens and pines. Many of these hills are now turning into summer residential places.

ASCENT OF THE ARAPAHOE PEAKS

The first of September we left Denver, about thirty of us, all members of the Mountain Club, except Dr. Russell, who was my guest. We went on the train to Boulder, then we transferred to the Whiplash, the little narrow-gauge going up to Ward and Caribou. We left this train at Eldora, and walked on up the pass to the Fourth of July Mine, about eight miles from Eldora. On the way it started to rain. When we arrived at the mine just before dark, it was snowing. The mines were not working, and the place was in charge of a caretaker and his family. There were other cabins there that could be used for shelter for the night and storm, but they had orders to let no one in them. After much persuasion they gave us the owner's telephone number. He was in Boulder. We got him on the phone. The custodian's wife talked with him and said that he would not permit the use of the cabins. Then I said, "Please let me talk to him." I told him "There are thirty of us here, and the storm is bad. If we have to stay out, some of us will surely perish. That would be bad for us and for you too." Then he changed his mind and gave orders to let us in. Next morning, we left at 8 o'clock and walked in the snow. It was not heavy, but it was cold when we reached the top. Dr. Russell and myself were an hour or more ahead of the rest. It was so cold up there we had to keep rubbing our faces to keep them from freezing. About ten o'clock it warmed up and we returned to Eldora in perfect weather. It was a pretty hard trip, but everyone enjoyed the wonderful sight we had from the top, where we could see over all that Rugged Range, for one hundred miles to the north and one hundred miles to the south of us.

ESTES PARK AND LONGS PEAK

Ninety miles from Denver is the Colorado National Mountain Parks, which include Estes Park, and the surrounding hills, with Long's Peak as the chief mountain of that range. There is no railroad to Estes. A railroad would pay well for 250,000 people go up there every summer, but the idea is to keep the place as natural as possible. The trip is made by different routes over the hills, but most interesting is the Thompson River Canyon. It is an easy grade for the automobile, and very interesting, cutting into deep craggy mountains and timbered hills, for a distance of twenty-five miles to the entrance in the Park.

The Park is the home of the tourists. There are perhaps fifty hotels there, with ample accommodations. All of the states in the Union are represented there. Roads to the top of the range and the summer snow are well-patronized, and the view from the new Fall River Pass is said to be one of the greatest sights in the world. The ascent of Long's Peak is one of the important climbs.

The start is made from the Long's Peak Inn, located at the foot of the Peak. This hotel was erected by Mr. Enos Mills, who came to the mountains for his health, and for thirty years he walked over that part of the mountains and became fascinated with them. He wrote books on the local birds and flowers, the beavers, the chipmunks, and the wild animals. It was mainly through Mr. Mills' efforts that this district was made a National Park, in charge of the Government.

At that time, I was a member of the Colorado Photographic Society. We had our atelier rooms fitted out where we did developing, enlarging, etc. While there I met a fellow photographer from New York. He was going around the country taking photographs of everything he thought would make interesting pictures. He was telling me about attempting to climb Long's Peak and had failed. He made two attempts but had not been successful - had gone as far as the boulder field but could not make the rest. From his description I got the desire to try it myself.

One Saturday I left Denver with a friend. We went on to Lyons by train, intending to take the stage for Estes Park. Arriving at Lyons the stage had left an hour before. The only way was to get saddle horses, which we did. We left them about six o'clock. It was only 26 miles and we could make it in four hours. A few miles above the town the road forks, one to the right and one to the left. We took the left side of the river. That led us in about six miles to the end in a mountain ranch and went no further. We were on the wrong road and had to go back to the forking again, then went on up toward Estes. Not being used to riding we soon got saddle-sore, the horses got tired, and we had to stop and rest. Daylight came on us before we reached the park. We arrived at Dunraven on the edge of the Park at about 7 o'clock in the morning, very sore and tired.

My friend was so tired that he laid down on a pile of straw and fell asleep immediately. I tried to wake him a little later, but he would not wake. I rolled him and poked at him. Still he slept. The 26 miles from Lyons was 38 miles, the roundabout way we came, and it was more than he could stand - an office man and not used to hardships as I was, and I too could feel it, but I was more sore from the saddle than being tired.

It was eleven o'clock before I could get him up. We hated to give up, but it was too late to make the Peak, which was 17 miles away. We had something to eat there and started back for Lyons. It surely was a painful ride, being already very lame. We finally arrived at Lyons just in time for our train, and boarded it for Denver; and so ended my first attempt to climb Long's Peak.

The second time I tried it stormed and I could not get near it. The third time was the charm - and I made it. Ten years after the first attempt we left Denver on a Saturday afternoon, headed for Estes Park, this time by automobile. They were now in general use. At 7 o'clock we were at the Park. We put up a hotel for the night, and next morning made preparations to go up to the Peak. While I was asking for information a young man, a college student, asked me if I was intending to go up. I told him I was. He said he would like to join me. "I have been here a week," he said "and have not had a chance to get in with anyone. I do not care to go alone." I told him to come along. That suited me. I did not care to go alone either.

We drove to Long's Peak Inn, about 12 miles. I left my wife and my two boys, John and Richard, at the hotel, and the young man and myself started on the walk up to the Peak - about nine miles and a 7,000 foot climb. At 12 o'clock we were at timberline. We stopped at the half-way house for lunch and left soon after. We reached the boulder-fields, then we met a party of four going up, and went on together. Getting to the Keyhole it was very steep there for three or four hundred feet, and difficult climbing, but we could rest up in the Keyhole, which I imagined was a sort of a level or flat place. It was not however, but a sharp crest - much as climbing on one side of the steep roof of a house, when on the ridge it is just as steep going down on the other side. Only in this case it was much farther down on the other side - nearly half a mile down, and at the bottom was a small lake. It was so far down that the water looked black as ink. Here was very little place to rest - only to hang onto sharp rocks, which I did for the first sight of the place made me dizzy.

One of the party we caught up with said he would go no farther, for "those little switching clouds you see there will soon turn into a storm," he said. That did not worry me, and I would go if it stormed. I started on the trail on that side of the mountain they call the Glade. In a very few moments a gust of wind struck at us. The little clouds swept by us like a sudden snowdrift and took our breath away. My companion said we should turn back. I said no - and kept on going. He turned and went back toward the Keyhole, and I kept going. When I reached the foot of the trough, I saw him coming back. He must have thought that as I had brought him so far, he should not leave me. When he got to me it was raining hard, and the lightening was fierce. We tried to get under boulders large enough to cover us, but the wind seemed to blow upward, and the rain and hail came at us like a spray out of a hose. The lightning was so close we felt the heat as it flashed by. This lasted about fifteen minutes, and the sky cleared up again. We were soaking wet, and water came down very heavily and hail filled the crevasses.

It was hard work for a while and when we reached the Narrows, I certainly never would have passed that place, except for my friend who was afraid of thunder but not afraid of narrow and dangerous places like this, where one slip would send a fellow to the bottom, one thousand feet below. It made me dizzy, and it was only because he went through it so bravely that I was able to follow after him. Then we came to the homestretch. This is a slanting mass of nearly smooth rocks, inclined about 45 degrees, and the only way to get up is by getting in the seams and cracks, where one can put the toe of his foot and creep up in that manner for a distance of 500 ft. or more. So when we reached the top I was about exhausted. On the top of the Peak we found an area of perhaps ten acres of boulder-field, great boulders dumped from the skies. If a cart-load of rocks were dumped on a level place you would have some idea of the appearance of the top of Long's Peak.

After walking around and viewing the country for more than 100 miles in all directions, we put more rocks on the monument that is being built there by those who visit the top. We did not stay long for it was too cold after being soaked with the rain and hail which fell on us below. It was freezing hard then. We had to hurry to get down - passed the boulder-fields before dark or we would have had to spend the night there. We got past them in daylight and down to the Hotel by 10 o'clock. We had been on the trip about 14 hours. It was a very strenuous trip, but one I do not regret.

Perhaps in describing my experiences in mountain-climbing I would make one think that it was too strenuous. It is hard work, of course, and takes energy to reach the tops of many of these mountains, for they are big and high.

Aviators and those traveling by airplanes can see the mountains as they pass over them, but not so well as we see them by slow climbing on foot, and I surely love to do it. If I could fly as birds do, I would soar from one peak to another, pausing on each for my soul to feed on the wonderful sights, letting my eyes rest on the lovely hues and the purple atmosphere which surrounds these adorable hills.

When I decided to go West I had not thought of becoming attached to these or any other mountains, for I did not know how great and attractive they are, but now I love them as much as I then loved the sea.

Acknowledgments

With gratitude to my Hume cousins, for allowing me to incorporate their father's foreword as well as the photos which appeared in his private printing of Bernard's memoirs.

www.ingramcontent.com/pod-product-compliance
Lightning Source LLC
Chambersburg PA
CBHW021951160426
43209CB00030B/1913/J